THREE MEN AND A FORESTER

THREE MEN
AND
A
FORESTER

Ian Mahood
&
Ken Drushka

HARBOUR PUBLISHING

Harbour Publishing
P.O. Box 219
Madeira Park, BC Canada V0N 2H0

Canadian Cataloguing in Publication Data

Mahood, Ian S., 1915–
    Three men and a forester

    Includes index.
    ISBN 1-55017-016-3

    1. Forest management — British Columbia.
    2. Forest products industry — British Columbia.
    I. Drushka, Ken.   II. Title.
    SD146.B7M33 1989   338.1′749′09711   C89-091503-2

Jacket design by Roger Handling
Typeset in Baskerville
Printed and bound in Canada

To Annabelle

Contents

Preface

One of the great privileges of my fifty-year career as a professional forester was to work with many of the province's outstanding first-generation foresters, particularly H.R. MacMillan. At the Sloan Royal Commission of 1955–56, MacMillan warned British Columbians that unless the province's forest policy was altered, the people of BC would have their birthright stolen, their standard of living reduced, their taxes increased and the forests that are the foundation of their present and future wealth destroyed. MacMillan's words are even more timely today than they were thirty-five years ago. Because they have been largely ignored and forgotten, I have written this book.

The laws and policies that govern the administration of our forests were drawn up by BC's post-war coalition government, a group that was primarily concerned with ensuring its own survival. Forest policy was established largely on the advice of a man who inherited the mantle of BC's chief forester — C.D. Orchard. I met Orchard when I was a very small child, then knew him when he was a powerful man in the Forest Service. I also knew other, more inspiring foresters who opposed the Tree Farm Licence policies he was instrumental in implementing.

Through the years I have witnessed a succession of provincial governments consolidate Orchard's mistakes. Today, the economic future of this province, which rests upon our forests, is in jeopardy. The very survival of many communities is in doubt. Compared to other forest nations I have visited and studied, we are decades behind in forest management and crop replacement.

Like most other second-generation foresters, I have roots that reach into a small homestead out in the vastness of British Columbia. I am proud of those roots and of my parents, who left their native countries because BC offered an environment for living denied them in the lands of their birth. Their story is a typical one: the pioneers who came to BC at the close of the nineteenth century were the backbone, heart and sinew of the vigorous communities that grew up throughout the province. They were the generation of homesteaders who served in the Great War and who survived to build this province into a free and bountiful land. Their children served in a second war, to protect the heritage their parents had forged. Now the ideals they fought for are being forfeited — not to an overseas enemy, but to a flawed concept of forest management administered with indifference to the legacy of the pioneers.

My father, a forest ranger, and BC's first generation of foresters taught me that foresters must adhere to a centuries-old ethic: the Magna Carta placed the forester at the right of the clan leader, chief, lord or king, and gave him the responsibility of protecting the forest. His obligation was to ensure the supply of meat from wild pigs, deer and elk, and to see that there would be sufficient timber for housing, industry and naval ships to defend the realm against invaders. The Magna Carta, signed at Runnymede, names the forester immediately after the judiciary and the clergy as a protector of the realm.

This concept of the professional forester's role was the heart of British Columbia's Forest Law of 1912. It began to disappear in the late 1940s with the retirement of field staff recruited and trained by BC's first chief forester, H.R. MacMillan, and his successor. By 1975, the principle had all but disappeared. At that time, the Forest Act was restructured to permit a politically driven, "sympathetically administered" Forest Service to selectively assist the corporate groups that now control over 85 percent of the public forest heritage.

It is my professional and personal opinion that if forest policy is not soon reshaped, British Columbia will become the Amazon of the northern hemisphere, or at the very least, the Newfoundland of Canada's Pacific coast. Our descendants will become poor folk whose heritage was destroyed by our folly.

I have long been sustained by my wife Annabelle, the chief of my support staff, whom I have courted since 1935 and who is "the girl" in my story. Through fifty-four years she has suffered me and cheered me in all of my endeavours. I acknowledge also the contribution of writer Ken Drushka, who provided research material and cleaned up my writing style. I am proud he has participated in this project.

IAN MAHOOD

CHAPTER 1

A Bit of History

When Captain John Meares took a deckload of spars out of a Nootka Sound forest in 1778, he became one of the first European loggers in British Columbia. Later exploring parties took more spars, but it was in the 1840s, after the Hudson's Bay Company moved its headquarters from Oregon to Fort Victoria, that commercial logging became firmly established in BC.

The 1840s and 1850s were the era of oxen teams and skidroads, so called because tows of logs rested on cross-ties, or skid logs, secured in the mud. Men called punchers berated the oxen and punched them with spears to get them angry enough to pull strings of logs along the skidroads. To minimize digging and hang-ups, other workers called snipers rounded off the leading edge of each log in the tow so it slid over the cross-logs. Greasers carried buckets of California petroleum oil and walked in front of the line of oxen, splashing oil on the cross-logs to grease the skids and ease the work of the animals. The oxen had to be fed, so oats and hay were grown in the homestead farms that had begun to appear along the banks of the Fraser River.

By the 1860s, sawmills were being built to meet export demands and the needs of growing settlements: Moody Sawmills started production on Burrard Inlet, and Hastings Mill opened on the south shore near Gastown, as Vancouver was then called. The province's fledgling forest industry began to attract eastern lumbermen. In 1876, John Hendry of New Brunswick and his partner, David McNair, built a sash and door factory in Nanaimo. Two years later, the factory moved to New Westminster, where it specialized in producing boxes made of hemlock, a clean, colourless wood, mainly for the salmon canning industry. Hendry went on to acquire the Dominion Sawmill Company on the Fraser River, east of Marpole.

Hendry was an entrepreneur with a global view, a man who planned early for the coming of the Canadian Pacific Railway. Knowing the railway would change his markets, he decided to position his sawmill at railhead, alongside a deep-sea port, to handle both rail and maritime shipments. Hastings Mill was the perfect opportunity. Owned by three Victoria men who were more interested in real estate than the lumber business, it had run down, but was ideally situated. Hendry purchased the mill property, timber rights and logging operations and merged his holdings to create British Columbia Mills, Timber and Trading Company. Included in the deal was timber around Burrard Inlet extending to English Bay, False Creek, Shaughnessy, Kitsilano and lands south to the Fraser River. The land rental was one half-penny per acre per year. Hendry soon expanded Hastings Mill's production from 65,000 to 150,000 board feet per day.

Meanwhile, the lumber industry boomed on Vancouver Island, and the pace of commercial logging increased as management sought faster ways to move wood and increase production. Not long after Hendry acquired Hastings Mill, a major logging operation was established at Rock Bay, north of Campbell River. Twenty-six steam donkey engines, over sixty railway log cars and a fleet of seven tugboats began marshalling flat raft log booms into Burrard Inlet. The age of railway logging had taken hold.

Many of BC's railway loggers had roots in Canada's eastern provinces, where men went down to the sea in sailing ships. Like their forbears they understood spars, rigging and skylines, and the best ways to apply power to winches. The skills of windjammer sailors were in great demand in big tree country: these men adapted steam-driven railway technology to power capstans, which were taken from sailing ships for service in the forest. The winch became a donkey engine and replaced oxen, and the spar tree, also adapted from the sailing ship, piled logs in a huge pyramid surrounding it. As railways were built, timber was moved in increasing volume. The skidroad went out of use, and greasers became chokermen who placed wire ropes around the logs. Trainloads of logs went to tidewater, where a flat boom raft was formed and towed to Burrard Inlet by new steam-powered tugboats. Clear-cut logging had commenced in BC.

The men who worked in the railway camps on the coast were cut off from mainstream society and family life. The camps were not even accessible to public view. Like the steelworkers who build today's huge highrise towers, these men were uniquely adjusted to a life of risk. A railway camp was a city where continued employment depended on moving logs out to the booming ground. Everything moved on rails—men in, logs out; food in, logs out. The sick and maimed followed the logs out. In all circumstances, logs out had the right of way.

By the end of the nineteenth century, logging was being done on a grand scale and Vancouver had become a hub of commerce. Manufactured lumber was being transported to the Canadian prairies to support wheat farm expansion, and shiploads fanned out to world markets. The greatest, best endowed port in Pacific North America would soon grow to lusty infancy.

In 1903, thirty-three-year-old Richard McBride became the youngest premier in the history of British Columbia. "Dicky," as he was known to friend and foe alike, was warm, engaging, full of energy and ambitions for his province. But on taking office, young McBride inherited an empty treasury and an electorate facing serious depression. The bloom had faded from the Yukon gold rush, and because oil had been found in California, Vancouver Island coal was no longer selling. Mc-Bride set out to replace the gold rush with a timber rush: observing that forest industry activity in Oregon and Washington brought a huge influx of capital to the developing deep-sea port of Seattle, he threw open BC's public timber lands.

For nothing more than a staking fee anyone, qualified or not, could obtain title to public property in unrestricted quantity. A man could go anywhere on public land, put in a corner post, measure a rough square mile from that post, and secure exclusive right to the timber it contained, paying only a nominal annual fee until the lumber was cut. As Martin Allerdale Grainger, an Englishman and second chief forester of his adopted province, wrote in his book *Woodsmen of the West*:

> There had risen a fierce rush to stake timber. Hundreds and hundreds of men—experienced loggers and inexperienced youths from town—blossomed as "timber cruisers." The woods were furrowed with their trails. Men in row boats and sailboats, small decrepit steamboats and gasoline motorboats had invaded the waters of every channel and fiord.

Most of the investors were Americans from mid-continent, where the forests of Michigan, Wisconsin and Minnesota had been, in the jargon of the day, "raped and plundered." To prevent more such short-sighted catastrophes, the American government had designated national forests, to be controlled by the federal government. The displaced plunderers headed for the forests of Canada. McBride was probably unaware that the white pine forests of the Ottawa Valley had already been destroyed, right before the eyes of federal politicians, by American capital that financed Canadian opportunists. In his naïveté, McBride had breached an underlying principle of resource administration in British Columbia: forests must be owned in the right of the Crown on behalf of citizens, as defence against exploitation.

There was short-term gain: in two years, annual revenue from timber licence fees increased from $140,000 to $1,300,000. But there was also acute long-term pain. Almost all accessible BC timber close to the shoreline and in strategic locations at the entrances to important valleys was in the hands of speculators, mostly foreigners. Public control was denied. The voters denounced the provincial government. Decried as a giveaway premier, McBride searched for a vehicle of redemption.

He ordered a Royal Commission on forestry, and recommended that a professional forester be appointed to head up a public Forest Service, as US President Theodore Roosevelt had done. Fortunately for the BC public, the Minister of Lands and Forests was W.R. Ross, who had the wisdom to hire as his consultant Overton Price, an American forester with experience in the Forest Service. And Ross had the intelligence to hire Martin Allerdale Grainger, a mathematician and writer, to draft the Forest Act of 1912. It was clear and conceptually sound, based on principles of reforestation and public ownership.

McBride knew that his redeeming chief forester must be a Canadian. Out in the back country, in places like the Kootenays and the Prince George area, the timber cruisers were restless. They were about to be denied their unrestricted right to steal public timber, cut it into railway ties and sell it to purchasing agents without paying any fee to the public treasury. A foreigner as chief forester would only further enrage that segment of the electorate. McBride appealed to the federal government to find him a Canadian for the job.

As it happened, a nineteen-year-old youth from Newmarket, Ontario had made a commitment to his widowed mother, as well as his school sweetheart, to graduate from the Yale University School of Forestry, and in fact ranked as the most outstanding graduate of 1904. The young man was employed in the off season by the Canadian Department of Forestry. On graduation he had quickly been snapped up for permanent employment, and dispatched to the west to examine lands in the foothills as potential forest reserves or federal wilderness parks. In his zeal to finish the assignment in one season, the young man stayed too long in the high country, where a winter storm caused his pack horse to bolt. By the time he got out of the bush, he was frost-bitten and one of his lungs was all but destroyed. Long convalescence in a sanitarium in the United States did nothing to improve his health. The Department of Forestry continued to pay his monthly salary, but then cut his wages in half. The young man could no longer pay his medical bills. The two women who loved him, his mother and his sweetheart, found an obscure French-Canadian doctor with a sanitarium in the cold Laurentian Mountains of Quebec. There the young man's health was finally restored, although for the last sixty-five years of a life that exceeded ninety years, he lived with only one lung.

Upon his recovery, he resumed his work in Ottawa and distinguished himself as an effective organizer and leader. When Premier McBride appealed to the federal authorities for a Canadian forester, twenty-seven-year-old Harvey Reginald MacMillan was dispatched to become the first chief forester of British Columbia.

There are those who say MacMillan was cast off by Ottawa as "damaged goods." This was not the case. His outstanding work history and leadership qualities meant he could have his choice of jobs. Furthermore, as a twenty-two-year-old, when MacMillan had taken the assignment as timber cruiser in BC, he had fallen in love with the province, and with the hand loggers who worked there: "the most hard working, virile, versatile, and ingenious element of our population." He may well have requested the position with McBride.

So effective was MacMillan's leadership that the conservative BC government came, ironically, to be regarded as the protector of the forest heritage. MacMillan's foresight in selecting men to head the field offices of the Forest Service was so impressive that the service emerged as a world leader in forest administration. Richard McBride, saved from humiliation and defeat by the young MacMillan, retired in dignity to England in 1912, as agent general for BC. King George V anointed him Sir Richard. McBride's name can be found today at a remote wilderness wayside station on the CNR line east of Prince George. There he is remembered for the "McBride Timber Leases," which nearly caused the downfall of his government and which were the forerunners of the Tree Farm Licence.

H.R. MacMillan and his contemporaries, including W.J. Van Dusen, Judson Clark and C.D. Orchard, were BC's first-generation foresters. Their predecessors, and to a great extent their teachers, were Bernhard Fernow and Gifford Pinchot, European immigrants experienced in German forestry. These pioneers influenced forest policy initiatives, first in the United States and then in Canada. They brought to North America a fear of imminent shortage of timber for an expanding population. Fernow thought of forestry as "a technical art, entirely utilitarian, and not, except incidentally, concerned with esthetics of the woods; it [forestry] is engaged in utilizing the soil for the protection of wood crops, and thereby the highest revenue attainable." In the tradition of the Magna Carta role of the forester, Fernow believed, as did first-generation foresters of the calibre of MacMillan, Overton Price and Judson Clark, that forests should be managed for people as well as cultivated for commercial crops. Sustaining the environment of the forest in its totality was important to these men: the concept was embedded in the forest law Grainger drafted. That law, advocated by MacMillan and his generation, was a barrier to politicians and their fixers who sought to frustrate the application of silvicultural science to crop replacement.

The job of first-generation foresters was made harder by logging practices established during the railway era: the clearcut method was anathema to a policy of sustained yield forestry. But there was little technological alternative until the late 1920s, when diesel trucks and crawler tractors, or bulldozers, equipped the logging industry with new techniques. Most significant was the fact that the smaller vehicles placed capital investment requirements within the reach of small businesses, in particular those entrepreneurs known as truck loggers.

The technology was now in place to eliminate two chronic problems: the vast clear-cuts and the horrifying forest fires that destroyed areas as large as the clear-cuts. With truck logging, the horrors of railway logging could be replaced with a powerful silvicultural tool — the professional business logger working under a financial incentive to initiate crop replacement. In Washington and Oregon, truck logging moved at a steady pace as a deliberate antidote to the damage of vast clear-cuts in the railway era. In BC, however, the science of crop replacement was all but ignored, and the province missed its opportunity to turn truck logging into a valuable silvicultural program. Vast clear-cuts continued to roll like waves across the landscape of BC, long after they could have been stopped. The Tree Farm Licence, first written down by C.D. Orchard in 1942, not only maintained but expanded every flawed forest management procedure established during the railway era. Uncontrolled and seriously damaging clear-cuts are our legacy, two generations after the railway era died of its own inefficiency.

CHAPTER 2

A Lifetime in Forestry

Like many immigrant pioneers, my mother was Scottish, her roots deep in Glasgow. As a child she had dreamed of leaving the city, living in open space and breathing clean air. My father, also like many immigrant pioneers, was Irish. His was a Cavan County Protestant family that escaped to Dowan County, south of Belfast, during a religious war. At age seven, his mother came to Canada with her family — nineteen of them, counting blood relatives and their children. In the late fall of 1857 they arrived in remote Muskoka, now wealthy summer cottage country two hours from downtown Toronto. Their wagon and team of underfed horses, rented from the land agent, stopped at a crossroads shown on a subdivision map. In fact there were no roads, just a demarcation where their meagre chattels would be heaped. Their land was rock-strewn and dotted with stumps of once glorious pine trees, and winter had already proclaimed its arrival.

In September 1900, my father was a fifteen-year-old boy growing into manhood. He was in Dawson City, a shack town along the Yukon River, having signed on as a cook's helper to a crew of surveyors working a federal government contract.

The chief surveyor had drowned in a canoe upset; the second in command, a political appointee not qualified to survey and incompetent in every respect, had deserted to join the gold rush. He left his crew leaderless, stranded, unpaid and deserted by officialdom. On that fall day in 1900 my dad watched a twilight sun sink just a bit west of south very early in the afternoon. He knew the Yukon winds would bring a bitter cold far more compelling than the winter darkness of Muskoka. He and one of the surveyors decided to occupy an abandoned shack, which had been the property of the deceased chief surveyor, some three miles from Dawson.

To call it a shack was to mislead. The poles forming the A-frame support had been cut in bush land next to the river. On the frame were shiplap boards imported from Seattle. Because grade 3 lumber comes from trees whose branches have yet to fall away, my dad's boards contained huge knotholes, which he would never forget.

Anticipating cold winds, he began stuffing the knotholes with pages from the *Boys' Own Annual*, an English publication describing to British schoolboys the glories of the empire and a stiff upper lip. How a hardcover magazine, its indestructible white pages filled with rich, glossy pictures, arrived at an unsteady lean-to shack in Yukon Territory, never entered his mind, even when its presence changed his life so profoundly. In the fading light, frost touched his fingers as he leafed through the magazine, scanning the pictures on each page before crumpling them for insulation. Suddenly he saw a picture of a young girl with long black hair. It had a silky sheen, even in the near darkness of candlelight — at least Dad thought so. He saved the page from the oblivion of a knothole. In the morning he showed it to the surveyor, who read him the message, for in those days Dad could not read or write beyond a few words essential for survival. The letter was an invitation for a pen pal. That night, by candlelight, he laboured through a response, stating his wish to correspond. That the hopeful correspondent sought a female was unknown to him — the surveyor had neglected to communicate that piece of information.

Twenty-five days after the unschooled communication was mailed, it was in the hands of Bessie, baptized Elizabeth, who would become my mother. The letter was an offer to be her "Pin Pale." She received two other responses: one from a girl in Dunedin on the south island of New Zealand, a more literate response that expressed a desire to have contact with the "old country," and a letter from a farm girl in Salt Lake City, country and continent unidentified.

My mother, aged thirteen, tossed the paper into her hairpin box and turned her attention to more current and exciting possibilities. Her father raged at her for trifling with her correspondents and ordered her to write apologies and seek no more pen pals. She went back to the pin box intending to destroy the letters and leave the affair at that, knowing that her father would soon find something else to rage about. Scanning the papers one more time, however, she saw the words "Dawson City." Having just read James Fenimore Cooper's novel *The Pathfinder*, she found romance and adventure in North America returning to her thoughts. America and the Yukon gold rush headlined the Glasgow newspapers, of which she was an avid reader. She set aside my father's pitiful communication and destroyed the other two items of elegant literature. It was a decision that only God in his mighty wisdom could have foreseen as rational and proper.

Soon a stream of messages flowed out of Glasgow to find Dad, if not in the Yukon, on the Alaska panhandle boundary survey, or in the timber staking country of BC — wherever surveyors performed their work. A comparable flow entered the mail pouch at Vancouver for return by the young transcontinental railway. At Quebec City, Dad's strange penmanship and sentence structure were transferred to the Cunard Line and thence to a three-room tenement in the core of Glasgow, then as now a veritable jungle of unhappy people yearning for fresh, clean space for both body and mind.

For five years or so Mother was a teacher and Dad was the pupil, growing more literate in each letter. She corrected his spelling and moulded his grammar to classic style. Her instructions were endless and intense. She assigned him books to read in two categories: the first to organize his composition and improve his word selection, the second to develop a smooth style of expression. On the list was Macaulay, once the Lord Rector of Glasgow, noted for colourful style and vivid presentation. Gibbon, the English historian, member of parliament at Westminster and author of *The Decline and Fall of the Roman Empire*, was required reading. So was Joseph Conrad. Mother told her pupil that Conrad had no difficulty with proper use of adjectives, verbs, periods or commas. In particular, he did not split infinitives.

By now my mother's interest in a lonely, neglected boy once stranded in Yukon Territory had changed. She was in love with her pupil, and he with her. The letters became great literature, expressing shared loneliness and desire as only lovers would dare to do. Dad, a part-time worker drifting from place to place, always in the remote back country where survey crews quartered, had no financial resources to reach Glasgow. Mother, her formal education finished, was denied paid work like so many women of her day. Her father, unmoved and unmovable, declared the only channel open for her was to go into "service," a word and situation she abhorred. To be a scullery maid downstairs, below ground level, in one of Glasgow's wealthy homes, was not in her imagination. She wanted space. She could never be confined to a dark dungeon beneath the street.

This love could not die. A tree had grown four hundred years. A logger had felled the tree. A sawmill worker had cut the board. The board had been carried up the Chilkoot Trail, each step an agony. A greenhorn prospector had used it to build a sluice box before abandoning both box and board. A knot, once a stem of a lush, green forest limb, had fallen out to create a small hole. Dad had happened to look at the pages of a magazine before using them to fill that knothole for warmth. For her part, Mother had simply requested a female pen pal, and page 232 of the *Boys' Own Annual* had somehow reached Dawson City in the land of midnight summer sun and perpetual winter darkness. Chance, which often is God's will, required attention. Mother would go to Canada.

Without telling her tyrant father, she signed an agreement to enter into service to the Patterson family of Burnaby. If she was to be in service, it would be in a vast new land on her own terms. Sir Clifford Sifton's immigration plan recorded a subsidy. A more worthy travel voucher has not been issued by the Government of Canada.

My dad met her at Field, BC, the eastern limit of his financial resources. After ten years of correspondence, they stood face to face, hand in hand. Two weeks later she persuaded Mr Patterson, a man of great wealth and even greater good will, for release from her service contract. He did more: he gave the bride away in marriage and hosted the wedding supper. He asked her to name a present. Her request, which sent him into hearty laughter, was that he send the Government of Canada the thirty-five British pounds it had advanced for her travel. Scottish independence would not be compromised by deceit. She would repay the Canadian nation its investment in her. She would be free with honour.

The couple departed on their honeymoon. The groom changed his rented attire, the first suit he had ever worn, for his familiar bush clothes. The bride wore a high-style full-length Edwardian skirt, set off by a richly decorated blouse. Her long black hair was shaped carefully on her head with many pins, and it shimmered in the changing lights and shadows. She could not know that this was the last time she would wear the finery that linked her to the Old World.

The honeymoon destination was Grouse Mountain. On the

walk to the north shore ferry, Dad carried a woodsman's back-pack with a tumpline around his forehead. On the mountain he was a man of the forest who strode effortlessly. A slender windfall provided passage at the first gully; he crossed as if it were a boardwalk on a city street. The year was 1910, the month September, my mother's nuptial bower a tent. In the moonlight, Vancouver, the Fraser River and its many channels separating the delta at the Pacific Ocean, spread in shadowy, shimmering splendour.

On that day, when my parents started their seventy-seven-year union of spirit, mind and body, the province's Forest Service was being formed, and Vancouver was a young city on the verge of becoming an inward gateway to the continent and outward passage to world commerce. But the Scottish bride and her twenty-five-year-old husband saw only the lights of the panorama below them. Their minds were not on the future of this province, but on Quesnel in the Cariboo.

What motivated immigrant pioneers to seek a home away from the city? Away from opportunity that even the most humble and least educated must have recognized? Why Ques-nel, a derelict town struggling to survive the collapse of a gold rush? Quesnel was 120 miles north of a transcontinental rail-way, 70 miles south of an uncompleted railway. If they wanted to run a ranch and grow crops for commerce, why not locate on a railway line that would transport the produce to market?

One answer, and it is a compelling lesson of the industrial revolution, was to avoid the city. The slums in the core of Glasgow were very much on my mother's mind. My parents wanted land and, poor as it was, Quesnel was land. For people born in the 1880s, land spelled freedom and inspired every sacrifice, every feat of endurance of the British Columbia pioneer rancher. Had the streets of Vancouver been paved with gold instead of wooden blocks made from Douglas firs, they would still have shunned the city. Land beckoned my mother and dad. They were bound for Quesnel, intent on growing potatoes and ultimately raising cattle on the flats now occupied by the Quesnel Airport. Their life was hard, but they survived their ordeal and the following years with every breath of their lives, which lasted a century. In spite of the hardships, they loved BC and they loved their land with intense pride and joy.

After two days on the mountain, Dad returned his rented wedding suit to the owner, a Hastings Street pawnbroker, and purchased two tickets on the CPR en route to Ashcroft. There he bought a saddle horse and departed on the long ride to Quesnel to prepare the house he had built, log by log, some months before my mother had arrived in Canada. In a sharp display of temper, her Scottish accent firmly audible, my mother expressed annoyance that she was committed to a location for her farm without prior discussion and acceptance. It was a mistake that Dad did not repeat in over seventy years of marriage — the partnership was to be equal.

Mother would have preferred to ride at her husband's side but she had never before been close to a horse except the huge, ugly draft animals that worked the docks along the River Clyde. Dad told her one saddle horse was all they could afford and, besides, the animals were untrained creatures from the open grasslands, while she was a tenderfoot from the city. He smiled kindly as he spoke.

Mother stayed at the Ashcroft Hotel to await the stagecoach that would take her to Quesnel. Late the second day it arrived and four fresh horses entered the traces. At departure the next morning she was assigned a seat facing forward. Bags of flour tied on the rear-facing seat, eighteen inches from her face, obscured her view and committed her to two possibilities: a bag would burst and cover her with flour, or fifteen bags would fall, with her at the bottom of the heap. Worse, she was imprisoned in a tiny space with the view to her left blocked by a large, thick woman and the view to her right obstructed by a burly man whose body smell advertised delinquent application of bath water.

Time seemed to stand still. On the second day, some fifteen miles from Clinton, the horses bolted, screaming in terror as only half-wild animals can do. The road, built sixty years earlier to serve the Barkerville gold rush, was deeply rutted. The lurching and twisting of the coach aggravated the panic of the horses and the difficulties of the driver. Pressed between her companions, Mother was pinned to her seat. The man swore incessantly. The woman remained silent, her body lurching against Mother, who prayed quietly. After ten minutes, which seemed hours, the driver contained his horses and dismounted to lead his passengers towards the flickering light of a distant ranch house. They spent the night in the luxury of a lean-to barn filled with fresh-cut wild meadow hay. After another endless day and an overnight stop at Williams Lake, Mother's seat-mates ended their journey. Thereafter Mother could see the passing panorama — rolling grassland, tree-clad slopes, trees, trees and more trees on the hills to the west and east. Days later, after crossing an uncertain bridge over Quesnel River, she saw the city of Quesnel. It was a cluster of shacks without particular arrangement. The front door of one house faced the back of another. A rickety toilet positioned midway between the doors was an obvious necessity of communal enterprise.

At the general store, so named as the only business to survive the long-dead gold rush, Dad waited with his horse and a borrowed buggy. Northward near Nine Mile Creek at the edge of flatland was the log house that was to be home. Mother would remember her first view of it as including a south-leaning chimney and one tiny window in the front. The window was under a sloping roof which covered a winter's supply of firewood for a kitchen stove, the only source of heat. Instinct told her not to pass through the tunnel of wood to a narrow, wood-planked door. She thought of the three-room Glasgow tenement where she had spent her childhood, of the windowless bedroom she had shared with three brothers and one sister. She stepped forward eagerly.

Mother entered her cabin, soon to be a home, on the twenty-ninth day after her arrival at Father Point, near Quebec City, where her immigration papers had been inspected. On the thirty-first day, her husband of twelve days departed to a cash-paying job as a cook on a road construction crew near Likely, some forty miles distant as the crow flies. He left the horse at the cabin. It was needed every day to drag a stone boat a mile and a half to Nine Mile Creek, fill a barrel with fresh water, and drag it home again. Dad worked twelve days on and two off. On the first day off he jogged the forty miles home, starting in the half-light before dawn. Five hours later he had a quick lunch, then spent the remaining daylight hours clearing his land of trees. At mid-morning the second day, he ran back to his job.

In her solitude, Mother made an inventory of her situation. Her home was a ramshackle cabin north of a town called Quesnel. Her furniture, built by Dad, was after the style of a Morris chair without any padding. Furniture could not leave the cabin unless her husband cut a hole in one of the log walls. Water was available only so long as the horse did not wander away to join the wild horses that travelled the flatland between the hill and the gorge of the Fraser River. Her steamer trunk, tied to the back of the stagecoach, had broken open when the horses bolted, spreading all her Glasgow finery along the Cariboo Trail. All she had was her husband, and the vastness of space. That she was in the vicinity of frontier Quesnel instead of Glasgow, fretting about what she would do with her life, was satisfying and exciting.

Two years later Dad had learned the basics of land surveys and obtained steady employment as surveyor's helper. His crew was under contract to locate and refine a route for the Pacific Great Eastern Railway, scheduled to be built northward to Prince George. But when the grade crew cleared a preliminary location camp on upper Nine Mile Creek, their sewage poisoned the water. Mother and Dad and their first-born, my sister

Isabel, contracted typhoid fever. Months later, discharged from hospital in Kamloops, they sought refuge in North Vancouver with my grandmother. The ranch was temporarily abandoned.

To make a living in North Vancouver, Dad pulled lumber from the green chain of a sawmill. In 1914 he went into military service and Mother lived with her mother-in-law in North Vancouver. Dad, a corporal in the infantry, was wounded by a hand grenade in 1917. He was discharged with every muscle in his back ripped by shrapnel. Mother struggled each day and long into each night to massage him and help him exercise to rebuild his shattered muscles. It was several months before he could work again.

Meanwhile, Mother had been scanning the Help Wanted advertisements in the newspaper. Unknown to Dad, she spotted an invitation to write an examination for entry into the provincial Forest Service. Again, unknown to Dad, she made an appointment to see W.J. Van Dusen, Vancouver district forester. He listened earnestly and with great compassion to my mother's request for information on what should be studied for the forest ranger examination. He gave her a gift of two books, *Forest Mensuration* by Henry S. Graves, who had been chief forester for the US Department of Agriculture, and *Treatise on Surveying* by William M. Gillespie, a professor of civil engineering at Oxford. Van Dusen also gave her copies of earlier examination papers, with important topics underlined.

Together Mother and Dad studied the books, read and reread the sample exam papers. Time and again, they crammed into the late hours. Dad passed the examination, and a few weeks later the family moved to Green Point Rapids, near Blind Channel, just south of Loughborough Inlet.

In Mother's view her husband was no longer a bond servant. He had responsibility for a forest ranger district, he skipped a patrol boat and supervised the work of several men — an engineer, an assistant ranger and several log scalers who measured and scrutinized the timber harvested from the islands in Johnstone Strait. She had advanced one more step, hand in hand with the pen pal who had responded to her childhood note.

Two years later, a promotion moved the family to Parksville for service in the mid–Vancouver Island Ranger District. Still later, Ranger District Number 1 in the Fraser Valley became the family responsibility, and remained so until Dad's retirement in 1950. The Quesnel ranch was abandoned. Now, seventy-seven years later, the crumbled log house is still visible on the right side of the road leading to the departure building. The chimney still leans to the south.

Forests have been in my thoughts and in my blood for as long as I can remember. In those days the whole family helped the forest ranger, and I was no exception. I worked with my father and my mother from the time I was a little boy.

My earliest memory is of an incident that caused great excitement in the tiny community of Green Point, our first posting with the Forest Service. Greeting the weekly arrival of the ship bringing mail, supplies and passengers was a ritual in which every resident participated. On this day, we gathered at the dock at the scheduled time, as the tide rips moved at dangerous speed in great whirlpools. The vessel was churning its propellers to sustain its forward motion against a strong tidal current, and it was somewhat out of control in its battle with the tide. I was a four-year-old arriving late for the event, and I ran down the sloping trail across the dock. Unable or unwilling to stop, I jumped into the battle between tide and ship. A bystander dived off the dock to rescue me. To him I am indebted for an interesting and rewarding life.

One Sunday morning in the fall of 1920, a Model T Ford roadster, with three men squeezed into its tiny front seat, arrived at our house. The driver was smoking, a detail I remember because my mother frowned on it so. He introduced himself and his companions as professional foresters from the head office in Victoria, and in a commanding tone he asked my father to conduct a tour of the surrounding forest area.

A debate ensued about the mode of travel. Concerned about getting dusty, the big shooters did not want to drive behind my father's Model T, a roadster converted to a pickup truck with a small, inadequate box. After considerable discussion, travel arrangements were resolved: my dad would drive and two visitors would squeeze into the front seat. The third would sprawl out in the box, his chin between his knees, facing the rear and the inevitable trail of dust.

When all the men were loaded, my dad said, "This is Sunday and I spend time with my boy. He can join us." With some fussing and grumbling by the interlopers I sat on the knee of one of the men who had usurped my position in the front seat.

The knee was uncomfortable and I was very unhappy. In researching documents for this book I was surprised to find that C.D. Orchard's memoirs described this particular visit to the ranger at Parksville. For the three men were C.D. Orchard, C.L. (Chris) Armstrong, a career civil servant, and J. Miles Gibson, who served briefly in the provincial Forest Service and returned to his native New Brunswick as dean of the forest school in that province.

On the occasion of my first encounter with Orchard, I also had my first visit to the expanse of huge trees on the Alberni Highway now known as MacMillan Park. The sight of that forest thrilled me then and does so even more today.

In 1921, my family moved to Ranger District Number 1, stretching from Westminster east to Boston Bar and south to the American border, then north to include the vast drainage systems of the Pitt, Stave, Harrison, Nahatlatch and Stein rivers — all part of what used to be one of the great coniferous forests of the northern hemisphere. As a youngster of public school age I spent many days assisting my forest ranger father as an unpaid helper. He was a fascinating man to travel with in the forest. He knew the name of every tree, and he could navigate and find survey corner posts and boundary lines not visible to a tenderfoot. He taught me how to run a compass, estimate the width of a cruise line, tally the volume in a tree and grade it, draw the cruise map and write a report. This he would scrutinize deeply, then he would correct it and explain each correction.

In those days the forest ranger was also the land examiner, the man who evaluated improvements made to the land by a homesteader before title was issued to him. Most of the homesteaders in the Fraser Valley, particularly in Surrey, Langley and the north slope lands near Haney, had their improvements evaluated by my dad and his young helper. If there had been an honest effort at improvement, there was credit to the maximum allowed by the office bureaucrat in the Victoria Lands Department. If the work was inadequate or simply not done, my father gave one warning: "I will hold up the report for three months, that is all. If you do not do your obligation I will recommend cancellation of your homestead." Usually the homesteader got the message. My father made few cancellations.

In those days, loggers were not required to burn their slash. Fraser Valley lands on both sides of the Fraser River were once superb Douglas fir forests with a huge solid wood content per acre. After they had been logged, these lands were opened for homestead pre-emption. The settler was presented with a quarter-section covered with an overwhelming volume of slash, and no equipment or financial resources to remove it. To occupy and clear land he built a shack, moved in his family and hoped a slash fire would not strike. He nibbled away at the slash by hand, sawing logs and digging out stumps with agonizing physical effort. In many cases, it took more than a decade just to clear the land.

The forest rangers of the day held annual conventions with the policy making foresters in government. At more than one convention, the rangers pleaded for compulsory slash burns by loggers before the settlers were allowed to move in, but the policy makers stonewalled the recommendation: "The industry would object."

My father, out of compassion for his client settlers, would pick suitable weather, go out in the middle of the night and start a fire. Many times I crawled through the debris to help him light it. Together we would rush home, load the vehicle with fire pumps and control equipment and await a telephone call reporting a fire. My mother, the unpaid office assistant, answered the telephone and gave us the high-sign. Off Dad and I rushed to the scene. He hired the settlers as fire-fighters and I ran the pump to wet down the settlers' home. We did a lot of slash burning for grateful people who admired the response team that "got the fire when it was small." Often settlers undertook to discover how the fire started. As far as I know, they never learned, but our fire-fighting efficiency was renowned.

In the same period, the forest ranger was an assistant to the game warden and was acting game warden in the hunting season, so my dad and I did a little hunting on the side. A friendly relationship with the game warden allowed me to work as an unlicenced guide for senior officials of the Forest Service who came out to hunt pheasant and grouse. My standard fee was twenty-five cents per bird. At that time my mother was quietly pushing me towards university, hoping I would earn a degree in forestry, and on game-guiding expeditions my clients spent considerable time selling me the professional forestry message. I met Marc Gormely, a peppery little salesman for forestry; Ken McCannel, who married into wealth and drove a fancy car, was my mother's idea of a role model. Another salesman for education in forestry was Bill Byers, a long-time supervisor of scalers who ran the scaling staff with the stance of a battalion sergeant major, a rank he had held in World War I.

In the 1920s, the forest ranger also wore a "special constable" badge and was called out to help the municipal police during emergencies. When I was about thirteen, a farmer entered the BC Electric Railway Station at Langley and took the station master hostage. The lone policeman called for help. The plan was for him to jump through the office window, glass and all, whereupon my dad would break through the door and somebody would grab the crazed farmer. I went with my dad, under instruction to sit in the car and stay out of the way. Dad, a big, raw-boned man, crashed the door. The farmer reacted to the window attack of the policeman by grappling with my dad. Locked in battle, the two men erupted out the door and reeled onto the station platform. My dad was on the bottom, so I jumped out of the car and started punching the farmer. By then Chief Macklin, the professional policeman, had arrived and the three of us were able to subdue the farmer. The station master was rescued with only a minor injury. I was thrilled to have fought beside my dad. That the girls took some interest in me for a time was a subsidiary thrill for a teen-age boy trying to prove he was a man.

Since those days in the Fraser Valley I have spent sixty years working in the forest and the forest industry. Of all my life experiences, my youthful association with the Forest Service as it functioned in the 1920s and early 1930s was by far the most instructive. Present procedures are far different from those of other public forest services in the world, and they are immeasurably different from the concept of accountability established by Chief Forester H.R. MacMillan in 1912, and brought to maturity by M.A. Grainger.

For field duty, MacMillan recruited experienced woodsmen and instructed them to patrol the forest. The ranger was commercially accountable for everything to do with public timber and land within his district. He had seasonal fire control officers, honourary fire wardens and a core of experienced on-call fire-fighters. Log scalers operating within his district reported to him so that timber taken from public property could be tracked and paid for in full. MacMillan also employed a staff of executive supervisors, who were not office-bound report writers but inspectors of field work, instructing and assisting the rangers — on site in the field.

What MacMillan sought and obtained was stewardship by the field staff, aimed at protecting the public equity in the forest. A test of his trusteeship system came when a forest ranger reported that a mill owner, who was also a provincial cabinet minister, was stealing public timber by failing to cause all logs entering his mill to be scaled for stumpage invoicing. After complimenting the ranger for his diligence, MacMillan personally delivered an invoice for the theft, plus the statutory penalty. Premier McBride was outraged. He demanded withdrawal of the invoice and removal of it from the records. MacMillan refused. As he told me years later, "I was twenty-eight years of age, standing exposed to political corruption, and I was not prepared to compromise my position of trust and repudiate my forest ranger who had expressed the accountability I imposed upon him." The staff of the Forest Service knew they had a leader who cared. They responded in kind.

The commercial accountability procedure faltered after M.A. Grainger retired and the evolution of some five layers of bureaucracy commenced. Accountability ended altogether when the ranger's office became so burdened with reporting to chairbound bureaucrats that there was no time for field work. Today the forest ranger is described as a district manager. He is an unknown entity isolated from the community, walled in an office, preparing reports that feed layers of bureaucracy in a highrise tower. He rarely sees the forest and is not responsible for accurately scaling the volume of harvest, minimizing waste in slash or preventing other abuses of public property.

In the modern era, in my role as consultant to business clients, I have examined field work and documents of the Ministry of Forests in cases involving failure to scale all timber removed from public land. I have measured public property wasted in the slash. I have initiated action to recover the equity of my client, who as contractor, like the public, is defrauded when public property is wasted and flawed official scales result in gross underscale — all due to the negligence of the Forest

Service. I have examined cost-plus contracts awarded by the Forest Service to major timber controlling companies for road construction, silvicultural treatment and other forest management actions, expedited at a cost to the public treasury. I see no evidence of accountability to the public land owner and a huge leakage of public equity. Even when flawed forest policy is set aside, public equity can hardly be protected: the administrative structure is crippled by its own weight and tangled lines of authority. An educated estimate is that for every forest ranger on the land directly monitoring public equity, there are five office bureaucrats who do not know the land and who are not charged with caring for public equity.

This is an appalling state of affairs to one who experienced the dedicated accountability of the public servant foresters in his youth. That there is no longer any system of accountability is one of the reasons I have spent years in the bear pit, seeking equity for clients damaged by the coalition between the Ministry of Forests and the monopoly that abuses public property and public equity.

Every second-generation forester, those who were born around the time of World War I, had family roots similar to mine, roots that reach deep into a northern coniferous forest. We are foresters who love British Columbia with a passion and who want to preserve it, because it is a generous land providing a living environment worthy of the struggle of our parents. We are the generation of foresters who experienced the introduction of sustained yield forestry, and we must evaluate what has been achieved and plan for the future in that context.

CHAPTER 3

The Dirty Thirties

I graduated from high school at age seventeen, in the middle of the Great Depression. I financed senior matriculation (first year university) playing lacrosse and soccer for a fee per game. In those days a picture show cost fifteen cents, coffee and a large glazed donut another ten cents. My girl and I walked hand in hand. We shared one great evening a week that cost me fifty cents. It was the desire of my heart and mind to win her. The competition was tough; it was clear I needed a university degree.

Most University of British Columbia forestry students in the 1930s came from rural villages. In addition to university fees, they had to pay for room and board in Vancouver and fancy clothes they would not otherwise need. More importantly, in my case, I had to earn enough money from May through September to support the project. There was no agency providing student loans.

While it is fashionable to say times were tough in the dirty thirties, I cannot claim to have suffered agony during 1932–

1936, my teen-age years in Chilliwack. We lived in a farming community that enjoyed underlying prosperity, thanks to retired wheat belt farmers who had sold out before the crash of 1929 and moved to BC. They ran mixed farms and knew how to husband their wealth. My parents and their seven children lived on an acreage, and we kept milk cows and chickens. We grew vegetable crops, fished for salmon on the Fraser and hunted deer and moose in the interior. In winter we shot ducks and geese on the flatlands of what had once been Sumas Lake, but had since been drained to create lush farmland.

We had almost no spending money, but we had enough to eat and we could listen to Foster Hewitt extol the virtues of the Toronto Maple Leafs on national radio. I played basketball, soccer and lacrosse and participated in regional track and field competitions with considerable success. I made a brief excursion into night baseball under the lights in Athletic Park in Chilliwack, one of the first small communities to finance night baseball and support a team in a semi-pro league. Many of the players were national league hockey players who turned to baseball in the summer season.

All four boys in my family were pushed and pulled by our parents to get a university education. My father offered me a loan, assuming that when I was established in a job I would then finance my brothers' education. I had no quarrel with the concept but it mortgaged my income, so I had a very strong motivation to go it alone. Many second-generation foresters financed their way through university by working as loggers, but in 1934, when I finished high school, jobs were almost non-existent. It was the bottom of the Depression and the relief camps were filled with unemployed men. So I was forced to stay out of school and scramble to make a few dollars here and there through the winter of 1935, until the fall of 1936 when I entered UBC.

In the spring of 1937 I got a job serving gasoline in a roadside service station, as well as playing for the Alberni old town baseball team. On the second or third day of work, before I had played even one game, Sidney Garfield Smith, general manager of Bloedel, Stewart & Welch, a great timber executive and a student of baseball, came in for a fill. We discussed baseball and, when I disclosed my interest in forestry, he hired me on the spot. I left immediately in the back seat of Sid Smith's car, employed as summer spark chaser and player on the company ball team. In the words of Sid Smith, "if you bat 350 and come back to us each summer we will take a look at you when you graduate."

The next day I was at Franklin River's Camp B on Coleman Creek, working on a railway that delivered logs to tidewater. I walked behind the trainload of logs, putting out the frequent fires that started when red-hot or even flaming coals fell from the firebox of the locomotive and ignited the debris nestling between the wooden cross-ties. But that was not the only cause of railway fires: the friction of the train wheels often peeled searing hot metal strips from the imperfectly aligned steel rails on the road bed. Fire frequency increased when a railcar was overloaded with an extra tier of logs. That first day, I put out three such fires. From my father's experience with railway logging at Harrison Lake, I knew I was in for a long, hot summer.

I could not let the girl know of my new job because she did not have a telephone, but I wrote her a letter describing the good fortune that would allow me to continue attending university in Vancouver. I earned $4.25 per day, six days per week, with board deducted at $1.25 per day. I was under a bonus of free board on Sunday, added to my paycheque for playing a double header every week, either in camp or town. I was banking $18.00 per week, and withholding $1.25 per week for coffee and donuts with the girl in the winter courtship season. I have long wondered just how Sid Smith convinced his accountants to make such an expenditure for a ball player. Indeed, it was one of the most difficult negotiations of my career, particularly when Smith knew I was getting about one-third the income working in the gasoline station, and eating from a menu that was thin on quality and distinctly light on quantity also.

The second day of work I put out a string of fires on the railway grade. Cars heavily loaded with logs wore the culprits. The loggers got another fire going that day from a wire rope haulback rubbing a log in the slash. Friction created quick heat and the fire spread with tornado speed, crowning through the trees to the top of the mountain and destroying a swath of prime, unlogged, old growth timber. The loggers worked only to save the logging equipment at trackside. By early evening, I was tired, hungry and ten miles or more from the cookhouse, a forgotten individual in a sea of space and slash.

To my immense relief, I was joined at Spur 18 by three loggers, also weary and famished from battling the fire. As each picked a stump to sit on, one man growled, "Goddamn spark chaser; every time one is on the claim there is a fire."

The stump sitter cursed me, the world and the environment of Spur 18. Eventually it was concluded that we should telephone for a speeder. This misnamed vehicle had railway car wheels and was powered with a Model T Ford engine that operated intermittently. Its speed came from momentum, gathered during its uncontrolled descent downhill on the shelf cut into the side of a deep canyon. There the vehicle bashed from side to side, testing the nerves and courage of both the brave and the timid.

The vocal one finally decided to go to the telephone box near the railway switch lever that opened and closed Spur 18. He lifted the receiver tentatively; the odds were five to one the line would be dead. It was not. An erratic buzzing rewarded his efforts. Stan Savage, the dispatcher at Camp A, refused to send a speeder. "Walking is downhill," he growled.

The response of the logger was phenomenal.

Stan Savage, not one to capitulate, repeated his growl with emphasis. Then, as an afterthought, he asked, "Who is there?"

The logger looked about, then counted on his fingers, two of which were missing. He reported, "Three men and a forester." The last word was a derisive sneer.

"Forester?" exploded a startled Stan Savage. "Who in hell is that?"

"Your goddamn baseball pitcher," was the logger's reply.

"Sid Smith's friend," muttered Savage. "OK, the speeder is on its way."

There I was in a sea of slash and fire-scarred stumps, with the clear message that as a forester I would be an unwanted appendage to the logging industry. I thought about my girl and an inner voice said, "You promised her to make it through school."

While attending university I kept my costs down by sharing a basement apartment near the university gates with two other forestry students and a man who would become a dentist. I contributed moose meat, a fellow from Chilliwack supplied turnips and we ate well. On the winter weekends I parked cars for Brown Brothers Garage, near the old Vancouver Hotel. There was limited undercover parking at the garage and most cars were placed in an alley or on the street. At the end of a function at the Spanish Grill Ballroom I would wait in the lobby, watching for a client who had parked a car. I took a quick look to identify him, and hoping I knew where I had parked his car, I would run to find it. Sometimes I produced the wrong car and the big shooter client got unnecessarily angry. But that was the 1930s; you did what you could, and since I was helping Brown Brothers collect a fee for parking space they did not own, they did not discipline me.

My forestry class had five professors and three students — one from a remote interior village and two of us from Chilliwack. While our courses would not be easy, we were confident of survival beyond the dreaded Christmas cutoff because we knew our five professors would not risk their own employment by failing one-third of the new crop of students.

The forestry content was crowded into the last year of a four-year course designed for those who took high school senior matric in lieu of first year university. We spent several years studying subjects we had already covered in high school, such as English, French and fundamental mathematics. Getting down to the science of forestry was long delayed. After some basic botany, slowly, ever so slowly, we got into forestry.

My senior professor was Malcolm Knapp, head of the Forestry Department. He had served almost from the time the forestry school was founded, shortly after World War I. Trained in the southern US, he was partial to railway logging, largely because of the grand scale of the machinery and the horsepower and ritual involved, but also because industry wanted graduates with a civil engineering background, rather than training in silviculture. To the major employers, even the Forest Service, mastering adverse topography was more important than replacing the tree crop. T.G. Wright, a graduate of Duke University in the southern US, was trained in the silvics of pine trees in Alabama. He was younger than his students in years. He was later to work for Bloedel, Stewart & Welch, serve at Canadian Forest Products, and retire as a successful tree farmer and land owner committed to forest crops. Other professors were botanists and dendrologists of quality, who came over from the arts faculty from time to time to deliver background lectures.

My forestry professors, while competent and interested in botany and the history of trees, were academics trained in the USA who had scant knowledge of silvicultural crop replacement for the species and strains of trees growing in BC. They also had little knowledge of, indeed little interest in, land ownership patterns in BC. Therefore they had little insight into the difficulties the professional forester would face when the land owner — the public — was represented by politicians who knew nothing about the forest and cared less. As a result, while scientific content was well taught, it was not interpreted according to the real world of land ownership, climate and land forms of the province.

In my view the forestry faculty at UBC wandered and experimented, trying to find a training course that industry and government wanted. H.R. MacMillan, too, was frustrated by UBC and spent large amounts of personal and corporate money to assist the department in finding appropriate educational objectives. I am not at all certain that this has yet been achieved and I share MacMillan's fundamental concern: too much time was spent on procedural detail, speculation and concepts, and too little on the scientific underpinning of crop replacement particular to BC's major species. In my days at UBC, nothing of the Magna Carta vision of the forester's role in forest management was taught. If this defect has been corrected, I have not encountered it in my contacts with graduate foresters, either in the Forest Service or in industry.

While it may be unpopular and even unkind to say so, I believe that the education of foresters at UBC got caught up in the sanctity of a civil engineering approach to forestry, which was a legacy of the slowly dying railway logging era. As a result, future foresters were not trained in logging procedures that ensure silvicultural crop replacement. I can recall not one discussion in university of the fundamental fact that where trees are grown as a crop, the logger is the primary silviculturalist, not the servant of the sawmill or pulp mill.

Not until 1947, eleven years after I entered university, did the BC government bring in legislation to establish sustained yield forestry. From that time on foresters have had the task of managing the province's forests.

CHAPTER 4

Railway Logging

In its early days, railway logging gave birth to a breed of men called hand loggers, the men who worked in the out-of-the-way camps along the BC coast. A hand logger worked from a crude float camp with a wife or mistress for a cook and several sons for labour. For equipment there were a few saws and a mechanical "jack," which was really just an oversized version of today's automobile tire-changing jack. With this tool and a man's own body, he turned, pushed, rolled and slid the logs downhill to the ocean. The hand logger favoured — indeed loved — steep side hills.

These men stood out in a crowd for their unique physical development and distinctive gait, whether in work garb or church finery. The men who felled and cut trees into logs had huge shoulders and thick arm muscles from constantly pushing and pulling long, heavy steel saws. High riggers who climbed the spar trees and "hung" the rigging had thick thighs and leg muscles like springs, accompanied by nerves like steel rope. These were men who expressed no fear of height or anything else. Levermen operated steam-loaded pistons, wild power capable of lifting and swinging huge tonnages of timber. Lean and agile in mind and movement, a leverman had a touch as gentle as a surgeon's. A hooktender, the jack-of-all-trades who bossed a crew, had a well-balanced body and the austere demeanour of a man who had to worry about the daily count of logs moved to trackside. Rigging slingers, who spotted rigging on the logs by voice signal, were thin and low to the ground. Chokermen jumped and tumbled like agile squirrels. They had the sleight-of-hand ability to slide a wire rope under a log where no space existed and in a deft, fluid motion close the circle with a choker bell. The centre of the log production team, they had long arms and walked with the uncertain, jerky gait of those who expect to fall face down with repeated, exhausting frequency. The whistle punk, in those days middle-aged, walked with one ear forward and the other backward, listening, poised to translate the rigging slinger's voice to an order to move the steam pistons of the yarding winch. He had the hang-dog look of a man who knew that one moment of inattention or a wrongly timed signal could be fatal to a comrade.

Railway loggers, with their distinctive, erratic step in which the forward foot explored the spacing of the railway cross-ties, were often perceived as inebriated and abused for it. Ladies of the night and hucksters knew better: the loggers' various physical characteristics revealed their spending power.

In camp, the men who actually touched a log were outnumbered by a host of others. These included grade crewmen, railway builders, steelmen, gandy dancers who tamped gravel around the railway ties and aligned the rails, enginemen, firemen, brakemen, cooks, flunkies and handymen. The engineman and fireman spent their working days stuffed into the steel cab of the locomotive, hard by the firebox and close to the steam. The heat was intolerable. In summer these men wore two sets of long johns as insulation against the steam heat. The warmer the day, the more clothing. One could smell a train-man, night or day, particularly if he was up wind.

If there was a demi-god in camp it was the forest engineer. He selected the railway route and the location of the production machinery. He chose the grade, designed the bridges and measured areas where the skyline could be raised for the airborne travel of logs to railside. He learned his skills mainly by trial and error, and if his portfolio of errors was not too large, he was qualified and recognized as a "Good Engineer."

The loggers regarded the engineer as a mystic who wandered into timber searching for space for a railway with a gradient no steeper than 7 percent — seven feet rise in 100 feet of horizontal distance. The loggers reported that home-finding was not an essential skill taught in university: the poor fellow had to put red flags on the backs of trees as he travelled so he could find his way back. This homeward movement started at about two o'clock in the afternoon so the engineer could record his field notes in the office. "The guy gets tired halfway through the day," the loggers sneered.

Completing the list of men in camp were shop crews, weld-ers, mechanics, cooks, bakers, pie makers, bed makers, hand-ymen, fallers, buckers, back riggers, flunkies, pumpmen, spark chasers, wood cutters, time keepers and a host of ancillaries, all of whom outnumbered actual loggers. Workers evaluated camps by rating the meanness of the superintendent and the quality of the food, the latter being of most concern.

The world within the camp breathed and throbbed daily, except on Sunday, throughout the year unless snow covered the logs in the clear-cuts. Almost all log movement was handled by steam-generated mechanical power, and was dangerous. At trackside there was a skidder, and wire rope rose to a skyline between two spar trees. These were held erect by guylines attached to a circle of massive stumps. From the skyline hung a carriage that was hauled out over the felled timber by pulling in the haulback line, and returned to the trackside by winding in the mainline. A set of wire rope chokers hung from the carriage and wire attached to the logs. The skyline reached first to one side of the track for some 1200 feet, and then to the other side for a similar distance. When topography allowed, cold deckers reached a further 600 feet to create a pile of logs that were swung by the skyline to the railway. Each turn of the carriage on the skyline was meant to handle a railway carload of timber, which, depending on the logs' diameters, would be three, five or seven logs.

When the action started, each man scrambled under the swinging chokers to capture one, attach it a log and jump out of the way. The rigging slinger gave a voice signal which was instantly, if not sooner, relayed to the whistle punk, who pulled a wire line to activate a steam whistle at trackside. With a blast of steam from the skidder, five huge logs were jerked skyward and literally flung along the skyline. Another whistle blast and the logs were lowered to the ground, within reach of a steam-operated loading crane that piled a pyramid of logs on the bunks of a railway car.

Short logs, regardless of diameter, and long logs less than 12 inches in diameter were wasted in the slash. If a chokerman hooked such logs he would "go down the road"—he would be fired. As much as 30 percent of the timber crop was abandoned to the slash.

Trains went off the track with distressing frequency. Official reports to head office blamed rotten ties not replaced by the grade crew foreman, broken steel rail due to overloaded cars, excessive speed or other frailties of trainmen—never worn out cross-ties, undersized steel rails purchased second-hand or gradients exceeding 7 percent to avoid switchbacks and reduce the cost of the road bed. Almost all derailments were the result of limitations or defects imposed by bean counters in head office who penny-pinched capital, repair and maintenance expenditures.

And forest fires sometimes erupted, started by sparks from

machinery or wood-burning cold deckers. Wire rope travelling at high speed over a log could start a friction fire; sparks from railway fire boxes and steel wheels against steel rails started railway fires, so too did careless pipe and cigarette smokers. Fed by the huge volume of debris and wasted logs, a fire could roar quickly across the valley bottom and up the side hill to the mountaintop, destroying more timber than was logged.

Motivation to work in a camp was strictly financial, an inducement which attracted otherwise home-loving men of quality. In the 1930s, with six working days per week and roughly 240 snow-free work days in the absence of fire weather closure, which was a rare event, the income was impressive. Depending on his job description, a man could make between $800 and $2,000. The hooker got a bonus of a few cents per log for his daily count. Forest Service annual salaries were about $720 for rangers, $1,000 for junior professional foresters and $1,800 for senior officials. The typical forester owned a house that cost $1,200 and had central heating and an inside flush toilet. The civil servant lived in luxury in those days. In the outside world, when men could find jobs, they earned between $400 and $1,000 per year.

In the railway logging era, silviculture was not on the agenda. The justification, when rational considerations were made, related to the words: "logging provides a paycheque not otherwise available." Professional foresters used the line to justify ignoring any form of silviculture aimed at fire control and forest crop replacement. In Washington and Oregon, where truck logging was operating on a much greater scale, foresters did not have such an escapist attitude. Progressive and precise silvicultural action by American foresters of that era are responsible for much of the forest harvest enjoyed in the US today.

In the 1930s, railway logging staggered through the Depression with its burden of huge camps and large-scale operations. Russia started selling lumber to Britain. The Americans imposed the Smoot Hawley tariff that all but terminated the sale of BC lumber to the United States. Disaster was modified, if not averted, when Britain abandoned free trade by imposing a general tariff on imports of forest products, while exempting tariffs on goods imported from nations within the British Empire. BC's exemption allowed it to drive Washington and Oregon lumbermen out of the British, South African and Australian markets.

By 1935, Bloedel, Stewart & Welch was making a small profit as the province's leading logger and sawmiller. Plans for a pulp mill to use sawmill waste and logs abandoned in the slash were on the drawing board.

In the same period, the H.R. MacMillan Export Company came under attack by Seaboard Lumber Sales, an alliance of sawmills of which Bloedel was a leading member. Their objective was to build an association which would, at the very least, destroy MacMillan's aggressive salesmanship in the reviving markets. This challenge pushed MacMillan into manufacturing and timber ownership in order to supply his overseas markets. Always a competitor and student of his opponents, he examined the Alberni area and noted a weak spot.

MacMillan eyed the rich Ash River Valley, north of town, containing more than a billion board feet of superb timber on flat ground that would be easy to log. He knew Bloedel was also examining it, so while Sid Smith planned and scheduled his moves, MacMillan moved faster. He went to London and acquired a form of option to purchase Alberni Pacific, the recently closed competitor. Then he went to New York to negotiate with the Rockefeller organization, the owners of Ash River. He obtained a right to purchase with a date specified for delivery of the money.

On the appointed day he returned with the money and closed the contract in a New York highrise. He shook hands with Rockefeller's representative and put on his coat. A secretary announced that a Mr. Smith of Port Alberni was waiting in the anteroom. MacMillan, preferring not to be escorted past the waiting Sid Smith, had to stand behind a curtain screening a lavatory in the office, while Sid was politely told the property had been sold to Alberni Pacific Lumber Company Ltd.

In 1952, at one of the first senior board meetings of the merged MacMillan Bloedel company, H.R. MacMillan, with some relish, told the story. Sid Smith, who was seated next to me, did not find the anecdote humorous. In agitation he stood up, bowed, said, "Here today and H.R. tomorrow," and walked out, slamming the door with force.

In 1937, the year I started as a logger, Bloedel was operating in the Franklin River drainage out of Camp B, and MacMillan operated at Nahmint, almost directly across Alberni Canal. In frantic haste, he was working around the clock to build a railway, reaching for the newly acquired Ash River Valley. He needed cash to meet payments on money borrowed for the purchase, or his bold, aggressive adventure might well fail.

Bloedel's loggers, secure in the strength of their employer, considered MacMillan's loggers incompetent upstarts with a short future. During the week, in the Bloedel bunkhouse, the lack of competence and virility of MacMillan's loggers was the chief topic of discussion. Baseball games between the two companies' teams were fought like wars. No insult or condemnation was spared. The bosses, too, led the ball teams as if they were engaged in military actions.

In those days, when loggers were men and women knew it, Alberni had two establishments of ill repute, the Goat Ranch and the Banana Ranch. In the former a logger could be stripped of his virginity and a week's pay in exchange for eight minutes of passion. The higher-priced Banana Ranch, with its reported warm environment and southern charm, allowed a full twelve minutes. On alternate Sundays, after the ball teams played double headers, the players often joined forces to visit one of the ranches, where all the men were equal. Hooktenders did not outrank the rigging slingers or the Oriental gandy dancers.

Non-discrimination protected the girls and enhanced the income of the Madam.

From the stories told by the girls, Bloedel's loggers assessed the prowess of MacMillan's loggers; the inside knowledge convinced them H.R. MacMillan had bitten off more than he could chew. History confirms otherwise, and the eventual partnership of the rival companies proved that pillow talk in the Goat and Banana Ranches was unreliable.

From Bloedel's Franklin River Camp A at the beach, a railway was scratched through the river gorge into Coleman Creek Valley. There, huge Lidgerwood skidders spotted on a railway spur reached about 1200 feet on each side of the railway line. Cold deckers, using wood-burning steam engines, reached and decked logs a further 600 feet. This ripped a swath of 1800 feet each side of the valley bottom railway. The slash was an angry mess of debris, including forty-foot logs up to twelve inches top diameter and quantities of low-value balsam and hemlock. Almost 30 percent of the forest growth was left to rot or to burn in slash fires that were an inescapable by-product of railway logging.

In developing the Ash River Valley, H.R. MacMillan established a policy of patch logging. This decreased the size of clear-cuts and maximized the recovery of small logs to reduce waste. Patching also reduced the intensity of slash burn and thereby aided natural reforestation by seed from the surrounding mature timber. This innovation added to the mileage of railway lines and dramatically increased the capital requirements for pre-production investments. H.R. MacMillan owned this land. He was a forester and he had no intention of abandoning a damaged and non-productive land asset of his shareholders. He even agreed to leave seed trees standing in the middle of a clear-cut with guy lines on them to prevent windthrow.

Bloedel's loggers condemned this alleged folly, but Bloedel was not logging on land it could take into title for value to its shareholders. Much of its land was public property where Bloedel would have no ongoing right — a major difference recognized by neither the logging fraternity nor government foresters.

MacMillan, though pressed for money to make payments to his bankers, nearly doubled his pre-production investment in railway and logging equipment because of the reduced size of clear-cuts. His creditors must have expected him to log in the cheapest fashion; not H.R. MacMillan. With an iron will he set out to establish good forestry, the first industrialist in the province to do so. This was a decade before public policy came to include sustained yield forestry on Forest Service land.

In my second season at Bloedel's, the railway logging era had reached its peak. I worked as a pump man supplying fuel oil and water to a cold decker some 1200 feet from trackside. One of my responsibilities was to lay two lines of steel pipe to deliver oil to the burner and water to the boiler. That required carrying two pipes, each twenty feet long, each weighing about forty pounds. Balancing one pipe on each shoulder, I stepped or fell my way over the yards of abandoned logs and debris. It was agonizing work in the heat and dust, and on many occasions I fell into the debris with my load. New sections of pipe had to be added almost at the same rate the sled-mounted cold decker pulled itself up the hill, sliding over logs, debris and slash. It was difficult to accept the huge volume of usable timber callously abandoned in the slash. And I hated the slash itself, particularly when I lay sprawled on the ground, an eighty-pound load of steel pipe pinning me down, entangled with a log some forty feet long. However, this was railway logging: exciting, frustrating and devoid of any crop replacement activity.

Not only was the work physically demanding, but I also had to learn camp protocol. There was, for instance, no orderly queue to the dining hall. Everyone tried to get in the one narrow door at the same time. In this situation, when the man in front of you is 240 pounds, the fellow pushing behind is 265 pounds and you weigh 152 pounds, your body squirts out of the line-up. You put yourself back together and go to the end of the line. There are 105 men ahead of you.

One evening, I washed up, changed my clothes, combed my hair and sauntered to the cookhouse just four minutes after the bell rang. I walked the rows of tables searching for a vacant plate and cup. Finally, almost in despair, I found a small place nearly hidden between two pairs of buttocks belonging to donkey engineers. Traditionally, those men ate well and sat down on the job long hours each working day.

I swung one leg into the space. The two pairs of buttocks squeezed against it, vice-like, from either side. I recovered my leg with difficulty and backed away. One hundred and five men stopped eating, which was rare. They were watching me. A flunky, known in the outside world as a waiter, was setting a table near the kitchen. The table had a white cloth and sparkling clean china plates. I walked over and sat down with my back to the kitchen door. The flunky rushed over, brushed my ear with an elbow and in an ominous tone declared, "Get lost, the boss sits here!"

Smarting from the attention I was getting from the 105 loggers, I challenged the flunky. More angry words ensued. The silence when the assembly stopped chewing, forks suspended in mid-air, told me my next move was important. I grabbed the flunky's apron and pulled him to the bench where the two sets of buttocks occupied three spaces.

"Get me a seat right there," I demanded.

Flunky eyed the buttocks and my closed fist. For such a lowly being to challenge a logger, even a spark chaser, would be a certain trip "down the road." The heads on the bodies attached to the buttocks knew that at the next meal, Flunky could leave them waiting for food or apply the unwritten law: Spill soup down the necks of unco-operative patrons. The space between the two pairs of buttocks opened and I sat down. The atmosphere in the room endorsed my action. I knew I had arrived, not as a ball-playing spark chaser but as a logger.

The desserts were now being delivered by Flunky: delightful chocolate pudding, cherry and apple pie and fresh, hot doughnuts. I sped to work on the sausage scraps, but not fast enough. The body attached to the set of buttocks on the left jabbed a thunderous elbow in my ribs. A greasy finger pointed at the chocolate pudding and the voice said, "Pass d'brown shit." In one motion my share of the pudding hit his plate and vanished in three gulps. Buttocks passed wind simultaneously from a low extremity and from his throat. He leaned against me, swung a leg over the bench and waddled out of the cookhouse. Never again have I been late for a meal in a logging camp dining hall.

In Bloedel's camp, I soon learned to position myself midway along the table nearest to the kitchen door, with my back to the flunky's line of approach. He then had to lean over my space to deliver platters of food to the centre of the table. I chose my food first and passed the platter to my right.

Experience also taught me never to take soup. Flunkies were paid $1.95 per day for twelve hours' work and no overtime pay. They allowed only 7½ minutes for supper. If you took soup, dessert was not delivered to the table. The employer encouraged such discrimination — it reduced meal costs.

The second week I was there, the cookhouse burned down, the victim of a store-purchased "tailor-made" cigarette brought in from town. Unlike the roll-your-own smoke, which was loose and well moistened so it stopped burning when thrown to ground, the tailor-mades continued burning. When dropped on the dry boardwalk planking and scuffed by the hobnails on the loggers' work boots, cigarettes easily caused boardwalk fires. Management did not sell them in the commissary, and tried to ban them altogether.

I believed it would have been more intelligent to enforce the no-tailor-made rule, provide at least four entry doors to the cookhouse and pass a regulation that no work boots and no work clothes were acceptable at the dinner table. But that was just a spark chaser's view.

Then there were the bunkhouses. A camp bunkhouse accommodated twenty-four men in two rows of single beds with thin mattresses and an uncertain spring base. The sounds of the imperfectly arranged springs, combined with heavy snoring and other noises of work-weary, overfed loggers, was not a restful environment for the timid person. One window opposite a single entry door was our air conditioning. Options, for which a consensus never existed, were four in number: door open, window closed; door closed, window open; door and window partially open through a series of experimental adjustments; and, finally, the normal, where a malcontent hurled a boot through the window. I noticed that 92.5% of all bunkhouses had broken windows, confirming that at least one in every twenty-four men is a malcontent in respect to air conditioning.

Bunkhouses were built as long, narrow boxes with peaked roofs, a design that allowed them to be moved on railcars. The exterior was luxurious, clear cedar lap siding, painted white — the most beautiful, rich wood in the world. From a distance, in bright sunlight and at the correct camera angle, the building would appear as a comfortable and aesthetically pleasing home away from home. That was an illusion. The interior was sheathed with a grade of plywood with open knotholes that exposed the dark glue coating on the inner ply. There was no wash basin or toilet, and no privacy. White cedar siding was not enough.

It crossed my mind that Bloedel, Stewart & Welch, a leading logging company with a well-earned first class reputation, had not progressed beyond the middle ages in respect to sewerage. Toilets were located a hundred yards down the creek. Access was through a fringe of timber, over a single, slippery log that bridged the creek, then up a path to a level spot some fifteen feet above the log. A shack was elevated over a pit dug in the ground. Spanning the pit, at shack floor level, was a single log named a Johnstone Bar in honour of the intrepid inventor. On it was space for six bare bottoms to discharge.

The call of nature came immediately after supper. The same line-up that had waited for the cookhouse door to open recongregated on the log crossing the creek. There was a compelling urgency to the call. Those waiting gazed at six bare bottoms spaced along the bar of Johnstone, as there was no other view. Each exposure balanced precariously and each in its own way discharged some shape and form of excrement. This was not mankind in his most appealing aspect.

Added to the lack of privacy and fear of falling into the pit was the possibility of being shot in the backside, or a more private part, by the waiting men, who passed the time by indulging in target practice. Using pistols and rifles they shot at the rats that waited for the discharge from the Johnstone Bar. Uncomfortable acrobatics on the bar were made worse by the plink of bullets and the screams of wounded animals.

It was not that the flush toilet and sewage disposal were undeveloped sciences. It was simply that spending money on the housing of workers ranked after expenditures on railways and machinery. Sewage and human comfort did not appear on the list. For every man at work, there were two men looking for work. The union struggled for survival and was a small voice dealing with issues more urgent than sewage disposal.

In my apprenticeship years I wondered about labour relations. But as a novice forester, I was much more alarmed by the failure to establish a new forest crop. Silviculture was not on the agenda of management and not visible in the activities of the public Forest Service, which had accountability to the public landowner. Experienced loggers and supervisors employed by Bloedel imparted their operative wisdom: Only on low-elevation flatland with deep moisture-retaining soils, where timber on unlogged rocky promontories could spread seed over the clear-cuts, would a new forest be assured. If there had not been a slash burn to clear the soil and remove disease-carrying weed trees, the new forest, if established, would be sickly and marked by areas of die-back.

The same loggers told me it was insane to log huge, wide clear-cuts in narrow valley bottoms with steep side hills. In slash burning, applied as a literal scorched earth policy, fires frequently escaped to run to the top of the hill, destroying more timber than was logged in the valley bottom.

This first-hand exposure to railway logging caused me to regard much of my university program with skepticism. The biological history of trees and forest management practice on privately owned lands in Europe and the United States gave rise to a nagging question: Why not in BC? At that point, in my second year at university, I was instead required to study French grammar and listen to a literature specialist expound on Shakespearean drama. I had to put in three years before I would study forestry. I was stunned and disappointed; indeed, I felt cheated. Had it not been for the pursuit of the girl, I might have returned to being a logger. At this point a hooktender's job looked very attractive.

CHAPTER 5

Survey — A Search for the Forest

In the years between the first and second World Wars, the extent and economic potential of British Columbia's forest resource was unmapped and unmeasured except by speculation, much of it so misinformed as to be misleading. Little was known of species distribution, silvicultural response to logging or the extent of forest acreage out of sight of travelled roadways.

The objective of the survey program in the 1930s was to map and record the timber supply in the "back of beyond." Except for the coastline, which had been plotted in the earliest days of European exploration, northern Vancouver Island contained an unknown forest: the maps for the area showed empty space. Similarly, the vast interior from the 49th Parallel to the Arctic was a blur.

The father of air survey in British Columbia was F.D. Mulholland. He had lost an eye in World War I and with it, the capacity for stereoscopic vision essential to examining land form, tree heights and other details on aerial photographs. This did not deter the intrepid Mulholland from working for the

development of air photographic mapping, which was in its
infancy at the time. He railed at and cajoled ministers, and even
the premier, saying, "We cannot wait for others. We need
technology for our mountain terrain and our type of forest
cover. It is silly to wait for others to develop it for us."

Penny by penny, F.D. mustered sufficient funding to keep
imaginative men of action like G.S. Andrews, William Hall
and H.M. Pogue exploring and developing technology. The
Okanagan forest survey of 1938 was the first project to use air
photographic planimetry on a production scale, both in the
office and in the field.

In June of that year, in the second season I was employed in
a Bloedel logging camp, a desert-like humidity level dried the
slash to an explosive condition. Elsewhere on Vancouver Island, especially near Campbell River, huge forest fires poured
smoke into the sky until the sun was invisible. Bloedel displayed
prudence by closing all logging operations. In foreboding silence, the Franklin River logging crew took the long trip down
the road, back to town.

With only six weeks' work I was unemployed, and probably
would be for the remainder of the recess from university.
Dejected, I hitchhiked to Nanaimo to board the *Princess Elaine*,
a luxurious CPR passenger ferry that loaded cars through a
side opening onto a lower deck. Once on board, I was welcomed
by the hearty voice of F.D. Mulholland, at that time chief of
forest surveys in the provincial Forest Service. He was a friend
of my family and he was on his way to inspect a survey project
in the Okanagan Valley. Apprised of my loss of employment,
he said, "Telephone me at the Penticton forest ranger office on
June 27 and I may have a job for you."

For the rest of the crossing, F.D. discussed the need for
logging procedures that prepared the soil for acceptance of
natural seed and, where possible, plantation of genetically
acceptable seedlings. An outspoken man with pragmatic views,
always forcefully articulated, he condemned the provincial

forest administration. His thesis was fairly simple: logging is the first step in crop-replacing silviculture; it is the responsibility of the forester as the silvicultural manager to schedule logging, dictate appropriate procedure and ensure the ground is cleared and prepared to accept natural seed fall wherever possible. It is also his responsibility to initiate plantation wherever natural restocking is problematic. The forester must be in charge of slash burning, for it is a silvicultural tool and requires accountability. Here Mulholland's voice, with its Scottish accent, rose in pitch to say com-MERCIAL accountability. Without naming any names, he implied the men leading the Forest Service had blinders on in respect to silvicultural crop replacement and that their forward vision was devoid of reason. "Blind as bats and stubborn as only foolish people can be," said Mulholland. In the style that brought him deep respect as one of the great BC foresters, he raged that it was a disgrace and a breach of ethics for a forester to stand aside and accept "ro-OOTHLESS" destruction and waste of mature timber in the slash. He said it was my generation of foresters that must stand firm against the greed in industry and the bureaucracy in government.

I listened intently and I still remember his wisdom. That is a tribute to F.D. Mulholland, because on that particular day my mind was on a visit with the girl in Chilliwack. I hitched a ride home on a milk truck returning empty from the Fraser Valley Milk Producers depot in Vancouver. My mother lamented my dismal prospects for the winter semester at university. My dad reflected silently.

The girl responded to my eager embrace in a decorous but thrilling moment of reassuring response. She whispered, "The Penticton ranger office will have good news." Her prayer, for which she had credits and I was in deficit, was answered. The telephone reported I should be at the Oliver post office by 5:30 p.m. July 2 to await the arrival of H.M. Pogue, chief of the Okanagan forest survey.

At daybreak on June 27 I bade my father farewell. He had driven me some twelve miles south from Hope to the departure point of what is now the Hope-Princeton highway. In those days it was an abandoned pack horse trail, part wagon road, built by the royal engineers in the mid-nineteenth century as a route to the Kootenay gold fields.

I had travelled this route as a fourteen-year-old boy, when I helped with a pack horse train delivering supplies to fight fire at the Whitworth Ranch near the US border. The fire had started on the American side and my forest ranger father wanted to investigate. He suspected it had been deliberately set on the Canadian side by Americans who wanted to destroy Canadian timber before they negotiated for land that would be flooded by a power dam. The timber was saved from destruction by the quick action of my father and his pack horse crew — an example of how the accountability system of the day encouraged the forest ranger to take initiative. A trapper reported he had heard some men in a beer parlour discussing a plan to visit Whitworth and light a fire on a particular date; my father investigated. We did not apprehend the culprits, but we did control the fire and save the timber.

On this occasion I travelled alone, my gear on a pack board supported by shoulder straps with a tumpline across my forehead. So eager was I to reach my destination on schedule, for fear the promised job would be usurped by another person, I jogged up the steadily rising ground southward to Allison Pass. My dad had plotted a map course that would take me away from the trail near the pass and keep me in the high country, until I broke through to the eastward side of the coast mountains. Then the travel would be downhill. From time to time I stopped to rest, exercise my breathing without the backpack and relieve my neck muscles of the pull of the tumpline. At nightfall, after munching an ample cut of roast beef between slices of fresh, home-baked bread, I wrapped myself in a canvas ground sheet and slept between two logs.

In the half-light of dawn I ate the second of the two sand-
wiches prepared by the girl. It was liberally spread with jam
made from sweet, dark red bing cherries, once celebrated at the
annual July 1 Chilliwack Cherry Festival. By midday I was high
above the Skagit River and could see its southern route as a
notch in the hills, before the flatland where the river crossed the
border. In the climb I had passed through the fir and hemlock
forest where a carpet of wild rhododendron in shades of pink
and purple grew on the forest floor.

Mountain grandeur and the sense of history of the wild,
formidable Allison Pass did not enter my head. My mind was
on reducing the distance remaining to Oliver. The fifty pounds
of gear dug into my shoulders. The tumpline chaffed my
forehead and soured my temper. I convinced myself, quite
illogically, that I was dropping behind schedule. My legs pushed
up and forward, pressing to destroy distance.

I attacked the grade, step after step. Years before, my father
had taught me that a man of the forest cannot capitulate to the
difficulty of the forest trail. He should not agonize or complain.
He should muster more and more determination.

I recalled working as a logger on a hot autumn day, struggling
across forest slash, stirring up fireweed spawn in a white cloud
that entered my nostrils and clung to my sweat-drenched back
like a sticky cloud of noxious gas. Then, with difficulty, I had
tossed aside frequent thoughts of quitting forestry and becoming a truck driver. Now, in Allison Pass, my mind said, "Stop
pampering yourself and keep moving. The other side of the hill
is a descent." "What goes up goes down," I chanted in a quiet
voice, at three-minute intervals. Then I spoke the words in
reverse to finish the sequence.

At last I reached the east-facing slope, where the underbrush
changed gradually to bunch grass dotted with scattered pine
trees. I triangulated my position with compass bearings on the
several mountaintops my dad had marked on my map. I was
well ahead of schedule. With a shout that spoke again when its

echo returned from the hilltops, I tossed the tumpline from my forehead and sauntered easily along a gentle downward slope. This was grassland scattered with pine trees, the exact number that nature, the supreme forester, determined the summer soil could support.

Now that the town of Princeton was within easy reach, only one night away, I rested to reflect on my situation. I had lost nine days' work at a net of $3.00 per day plus $1.25 for two Sundays of ball-playing bonus. This did not include my log count bonus for the days I set chokers for the hook tender. I estimated a loss of $29.50, equal to six weeks' room and board during the fall university semester. The survey job paid only $2.50 per day six days per week, a net loss of about fifty cents per day for 100 days, a further loss $50.00. My total economic setback would be about $80.00, not counting the $1.25 per week I was saving for coffee and donuts with the girl.

That night I slept in the pine forest, waking several times worried about my projected financial shortfall. In the morning the air was so hot and still, the pine needles so dry, that I ate a fireless breakfast of cold beans and two slices of bread. That night I stopped to rest in a field where fresh-cut hay was stacked, and for supper I "borrowed" ripe tomatoes from a farmer's field. The tomato juice moistened the heel of the girl's homemade bread, now crushed and dry from difficult travel. I was elated. With only a few miles to go, I was on schedule to have breakfast in Princeton on June 30.

The next morning, I spent thirty-five cents on a breakfast of porridge, ham and eggs, hash browns and a glass of milk. In front of the cafe, a lone truck was parked. The driver, Syd Millar, a youth of my age, planned to take a load of pre-cut ponderosa pine apple box lumber to Penticton. He welcomed me as passenger and helper.

Syd, a track and field athlete, recognized me as a sprinter and middle distant participant in coastal track meets. He urged me to enter an invitational track and field meet in Penticton the next day. There were to be cash prizes, as was common in those days: first place $10.00, second $7.00 and third $3.50. At noon we arrived in Penticton with registration priority. To avoid opposition to an uninvited competitor from the coast, Syd registered me as a resident of Oliver under an assumed name and, hence, a local novice eligible to compete.

The preliminary heats in the sprints indicated there was tough competition from interior and US runners. My new friend Syd won three events and placed second in another. Under my temporary name, I placed first in the 100- and 220-yard sprints, second in the broad jump and first in the half-mile. I entered this race, the last of the day, because there were no preliminary heats and because I had once run this distance. I had placed third to William Dale of Victoria and Mansfield Beach of Vancouver, who had tied for a time that was, in its day, a BC record.

My cash winnings were $30.50. I had recovered nearly half the income I had lost in the transition from logger to Forest Service employee. By delaying my return to university for a week or so I would strengthen my financial larder even further. There was merit in being a forest surveyor.

My friend Syd Millar, in gratitude for a successful day of foot racing, delivered me to the post office at Oliver two hours before my appointment with the Forest Service. The wait was long, and I was to learn Pogue was famous for never being on time for a meeting and never failing to appear with a plausible but convoluted explanation.

I could not foresee that meeting him would lead to an adventure in an unexpected war, nor did I suspect he would marry a sister of the girl and become my brother-in-law, sharing a family relationship that would exceed fifty years. I did not yet know that my life as a forester would be much more exciting because of Pogue and his distinctive Irish charm.

Here was a man who always declared a project impossible, then attacked it without a plan and succeeded where those who planned would often fail. On one occasion, when he was at White Swan lake in the Rockies and forty miles by pack horse trail from the main Invermere-Cranbrook highway, he had to get to an important meeting in Victoria. Undaunted, he jogged along the trail through the night and hitchhiked to Nelson, where he had stored his car. In those days, traffic was infrequent and one could expect to wait hours for a ride. But not an Irishman. Ten minutes after Pogue arrived at the highway, a driver heading south was flagged down and persuaded to drive to Nelson instead. After Pogue's car was retrieved, there was a wild, nonstop drive via Wenatchee, across Washington, through Everett and over to the Olympic Peninsula to the ferry that crossed to Victoria.

Pogue arrived twenty-two minutes late. F.S. MacKinnon, head of surveys and a Scot, listened patiently to a convoluted apology and responded, "No problem, Mickey, your meeting with me is tomorrow. But please stay, you will make a contribution to this meeting." To this day Pogue does not know whether he was, in fact, a day early for his meeting. In any event, the meeting scheduled for the next day was not convened.

On that July day at Oliver, Pogue was late, but I saw him coming two hours before his arrival. There was a trail of dust that started on a distant hillside to the east and rose like a vapour trail in a cloudless sky. It tracked the path of a vehicle heading determinedly to the main square of Oliver where it stopped not at the post office, but at the liquor store. Four doors opened in unison and out scrambled seven voices that shouted, in unison, "Are you Mahood?" Before I could respond, the voices directed a more important question, "Do we get two gallons of rum or one?" There was no pause before the voices answered themselves in unison: "Two."

A small man flashing a smile said, "If you are Mahood, come on over. There are seven of us and we are one man short." I was to learn that behind that smile was a disciplined toughness and a determination to get a job done. He demanded and was willingly given one hundred percent energy output in executing the miles of cruise line he scheduled each day. "Do not bother to explain why you did not cover the ground, just show me on the air photograph where you ended the strip line. I will tell you if I am satisfied with the mileage you travel each day."

Thirty overproof rum, brown and rich, was the potion of the surveyor. It was not a stimulant to fuel the incessant demand for strip mileage, but the quaff, every second weekend in town, that would replenish the driving energy consumed day after day in the bush. Pogue had an extrasensory perception of when a crew was tired: it might be ten continuous days in the bush, or twelve days if he was behind his self-imposed schedule. He knew, and he alone determined when it was time to recharge the batteries in town.

The two gallons of rum were held tenderly, one in the lap of Jack Mottishaw, Berlin Olympic athlete, the other in the fatherly arms of middle-aged George Silburn, master surveyor. Silburn schooled a long list of future foresters who otherwise would not have found their way back to camp from one of Pogue's pre-plotted strips in the back country. Silburn mothered and fathered the trainees to curb any wayward leanings.

With eight men and two jugs of rum in the station wagon, Pogue, in a tone of command, said, "Supper, wash — then to dance at the Corral." By 7:30 p.m., only forty-five minutes after its dusty arrival, the station wagon stopped at an open-air dance floor built over the lake. Its entryway was two planks laid six inches apart, with no guard rails. The water was deep, and thick with reeds that would entangle anyone who might fall due to unnatural causes.

After the dancing, there would be ample opportunity for the development of meaningful relationships. Committed to the girl, I made a note to proceed with caution. Seven innocent young men walked the plank, followed by the stabilizing, mature wisdom of George Silburn, our self-appointed chaperone. Mottishaw strode past the keeper of the plank entrance, saying, "Pogue pays." In sequence, each surveyor did likewise. Pogue, the last to enter, offered a backward point of the right thumb, saying, "Pogue pays." As we entered the hall, gay, laughing young ladies watched us. Others among them were not so young. I assumed they were chaperones on guard, but I soon noticed that their motives were somewhat less noble and distinctly more predatory.

It was the age of the "Big Apple," an undisciplined formation which, open to innovative fancy, mingled square dance, highland fling and, from time to time, an intimate waltz, depending on the sobriety and passion exhibited by the dancers. The orchestra leader, who was also the owner of the Corral, was adept at perceiving relationships among his clients.

Suddenly the music stopped and the saxophone-playing proprietor began a search for Pogue. Angry words and a pushing match ensued, with bodies ending up on the floor. Concerned about my duty to my new associates, I moved forward to assist Pogue. An arm pulled me back. It was owned by Silburn, who whispered, "It's all part of the warm-up act. Pogue does pay and he gets a discount on behalf of the crew, depending on crowd size."

"Why?" I asked.

"Figure it out," said Silburn. "We come to town every couple of weeks and spend some money. All the girls, including some mothers, come to dance. This town was broke in the Depression, free-spending foresters employed by the government are great. The girls love it and so do their mothers."

"Pogue told me I was to pay him," I responded. "Is he taking a fee?"

Silburn gave a hearty laugh. "No! Pogue was telling you he will charge the discounted price on your commissary account. In case you do not know it, the two gallons of rum are paid for by the dance hall proprietor and recorded as a credit to your commissary — so go dance the night away."

As the dance progressed, the girls encouraged Mottishaw, a fine singer. He borrowed a guitar and sang, soft soul music. Allan Dixon, a future district forester, sang an aria from Aïda, in a rich tenor. Pogue, who could not sing a note, offered a rendition of "St. Louis Woman." It was more of an amiable monologue made acceptable with assistance from the audience when Pogue got off key or forgot the lines, which was frequent.

The finale of the Forest Survey's floor show was the participatory mass production of the "Oliver Corral Big Apple of 1938." The home waltz, when it came, lasted more than an hour, until the inebriated, enterprising proprietor-musician eased himself slowly to the floor with his tenor saxophone for a pillow.

In the winter of 1938-39 I was granted a ten-day recess from university to work in Victoria, with pay, assisting in the compilation of maps and tabulation of data gathered during the previous summer. My income from logging and surveying in the summer, plus the unexpected office work, gave me a budget surplus. I could buy the girl a Christmas present.

In the summer of 1939 I was hired again, and promoted to the coveted job of cruiser, with a 25 percent increase in pay. The crew surveyed the entire northern third of Vancouver Island, unmapped except for the shoreline traversed by early explorers. The underbrush and dense salal as high as our armpits tested our endurance. Pogue demanded and got more miles of survey strip than in the open grasslands of the interior pine forest. At the end of many days, I lay exhausted at the shoreline, waiting to be picked up by the power boat.

At one point I made a decision to tell Pogue to dump it, I would go back to logging. But I could never utter the words. My training taught me that a man of the forest is never defeated by the forest. Moreover, while Pogue drove his crew and pushed them, he also pushed himself. In my moments of exhaustion I told myself, "If that guy can do it, so can I."

On one occasion I thought I had him cold. We were crossing

from the mouth of Mahatta River to set up a "Y camp," a temporary work centre. This involved backpacking the steep country from the beach. Pogue and the engineer of the *BC Forester*, our seventy-foot floating home-away-from-home, were commandeered to carry supplies up the hill. My compassman and I were conditioned to the work. Pogue, office-bound from plotting air photographs and monitoring schedules, was not hardened to field work. To induce him to exercise compassion in scheduling our daily travel, I placed fifteen pounds of white painted rocks in the pack load I prepared for him. In bulk it was smaller than mine, and I knew he would not, for that reason, complain about the weight.

A few hours into the day, the engineer was exhausted and his backpack was split for distribution to others. Pogue took a full share. I noticed he was struggling a little bit, but he never said a word or asked for a rest. We kept moving. By midday, after five hours of steady travel, we were at the top of the hill at our campsite. We unpacked our loads and stored the food and equipment before going back down the mountain. Before descending I looked to see if Pogue had put the white rocks in the food storage cairn. He had not. I noticed his empty pack was somewhat bulky, but I asked no questions. On our arrival at the beach, where the ship swung at anchor, Pogue, with austere solemnity, removed his backpack, withdrew the three white painted rocks and replaced them on the beach without comment. He turned and saluted me in military style and boarded the vessel. There were no more complaints about size or weight of backpacks or the length of cruise line allotted each day.

Then the world changed. In August 1939 it went to war.

Deep in the rain forest of northern Vancouver Island, out of touch with the world outside, we had scanty information on events far from British Columbia. In late September, as we relaxed in the forward cabin of the *BC Forester*, the agony imposed on Poland by Nazi armies threw a chill over our conversation. Each man knew that our generation would go to war, just as our fathers' had done.

John LeMare, a timber cruiser and forest engineering undergraduate living in Duncan, was a man with big feet, a big body and a big heart to go with it. "Hell no!" he said. "Europeans can solve their own problems. I stay home." Weeks later, when the intensity of Nazi brutality could not be ignored, John changed his mind. He went to war immediately and was one of the first of the survey group to enlist. Before a year passed, he died in active service, becoming the first of his classmates and many Forest Service associates to make that sacrifice. When he returned from air force duty, Pogue named LeMare Lake in honour of big John. It is on Vancouver Island, west of Port MacNeil and near the restless Pacific surf.

On that homeward journey, I did not join in the discussion. I had a father who had been wounded by a hand grenade in the first World War. I had two lifelong friends who had lost their father to the same war. For a decade we had been brought up as brothers, sharing my dad at our summer camp and on trips into the forest. I had experienced their loneliness. I had no interest in soldiering.

I told my friends it would be a long war and there was no rush to get in. "Wait until we finish our university education," I said. "If it is to be a long war Canada will wait for us." Behind that logic was my personal agenda: I would finish university, and marry the girl I had loved and courted since my seventeenth year. Then I would go to war. Already I had two years' service as a military cadet in the university officers training corps. I needed two more semesters to finish my degree in forestry. Unless officialdom called me for other purposes, that was my schedule.

There was no response from my fellow travellers in the *BC Forester*. The future was so uncertain that nothing could be said in agreement or disagreement, and no one wanted to disclose any hint of patriotic delinquency. Each of us knew that when duty called, despite personal plans, even against our parents' advice, we would say yes to a call from our country.

The girl, to ensure I would not unilaterally change my plans, agreed to marry me immediately after I graduated. Pogue, rich with poker winnings extracted from the engineering and chemical staff of the Port Alice pulp mill, loaned me sufficient money for an engagement ring. My own resources were divided equally among seven envelopes for seven months of university expenses. Besides, some of the money from the pulp mill staff was mine—I had dealt Pogue the buried ace in his winning hand of stud poker. To repay the loan I pledged Pogue all my officers training income, and the rascal accepted. With three nights a week and every Saturday afternoon devoted to training, Pogue soon got his money.

CHAPTER 6

Then to Soldier

From October 1939 through April 1941, the final two years of my double degree course were physically, intellectually and logistically challenging. Traditionally, a forestry degree was earned from the applied science faculty and included a specialization in civil engineering, with a brief discussion of silvicultural crop replacement tossed in. This qualified graduates to build roads, bridges, railways and sewage systems. I was reluctant to study the design of sewers; I wanted to make my contribution to society by helping to sustain a healthy forest environment.

Because of that desire I became the first undergraduate to sidestep engineering and substitute a degree in commerce, involving financial planning and business administration, so that I could learn how to find the money required for a good silviculture program. When the shock waves from this innovation rumbled through the forestry profession, nothing but failure and a life of misery was forecast for a man with such a mediocre intellect as to abandon engineering. It was predicted there would be no room for me at the inn.

I did not agonize over such sombre prophesies. I was convinced railway logging was on the way out, and my exposure to it had told me I must apply the biological science of forest management. From my perspective, linking commerce and forestry was prudent. In retrospect, it has been not only prudent but rewarding.

The path I pioneered was difficult, however, for both practical and philosophical reasons. The commerce faculty was housed a great distance from the civil engineering buildings where forestry lectures were given, so it was a logistical nightmare to dash between the two centres. I solved the problem by purchasing a high-speed bicycle. Then there was the added burden of military affairs. In 1937 I had volunteered to enter the Canadian Officers Training Corps, which had a militia unit at UBC. I had no zeal to be a soldier; my primary interest was financial. There was income for a militia member. While my military skills were immature, I could march back and forth on the parade square, keep in step and salute with appropriate decorum. These appeared to be the only criteria that qualified one as "officer material."

In the spring of 1940 the COTC came out of the closet and all male university students attended regular Saturday parades. We marched back and forth, eyes righting to salute people. It was frustrating to spend a Saturday sloping arms by numbers when the important thing to do was visit the girl in Chilliwack. Because of the alphabetic proximity of his surname, Brud Matheson stood next me in the weekly military parade. Brud was a basketball and lacrosse star, who would later become a senior executive at Crown Zellerbach. We reached an agreement: on alternate Saturday mornings I would collapse on the parade square in a dead faint. He would jump to my assistance and help me to the medical centre, where I would be excused from the parade. That would get me to Chilliwack. The next week Brud, who had a romantic interest of his own, would be the casualty. In war one must do what he has to do.

At the end of April 1941 when I completed my final examinations, I delivered my thesis paper to Professor Malcolm Knapp, the father confessor to a long list of second-generation foresters, and bade farewell to my two classmates. My next action was to toss my textbooks from the Burrard Bridge into False Creek. I then travelled to New Westminster on the BC Electric Interurban, and walked to Maillardville to report for work in the Canadian Western Lumber Company Plywood plant at Fraser Mills. I had a job as assistant to the manager, monitoring quality control in the transition from cold pressing to hot press bonding of plywood — then a new technology. The plant operated three shifts turning out structural, housing and packaging goods for the military needs of a world at war.

On my first day off work I went to Chilliwack to visit the girl. True to our compact, I had graduated from university. We were married October 4, 1941. My mother loaned us her Austin for a four-day honeymoon to Shuswap Lake. That same month I volunteered for enlistment in the Westminster Regiment. I waited for a call-up through the vagaries of military procedures, and was eventually ordered to officers training at Gordon Head, Victoria, where I graduated as an engineer officer.

By late 1942 I was stationed at Chilliwack, training raw recruits in the art of bridge building. Using steel sections that a team of men carried on a dead run, we paused to lock the components together with pins and then cantilevered the bridge into position across a stream. This was the famous Bailey bridge that was eventually to span every canal and river in northern Europe, many of them constructed under aircraft strafing, mortar and rifle fire.

A modern army moves by the sweat, toil and strong backs of the Military Engineering units. Often they work out front of the infantry and experience heavy casualties removing land mines or building assault bridges. At Chilliwack we also taught mine laying on roads and bridges. We instructed students in building demolition, and taught the risky work of defusing the kind of live bombs placed on railways and in roads where men and vehicles travelled.

I taught defensive rifle shooting as well as what persons in high command considered most important: marching in step. Many of the recruits were ex-loggers. If the powers that be had ever worked in the forest, they would know the difficulty of teaching a railway logger to take two consecutive steps of the same length and rhythm, and they might have been willing to accept less than perfect marching by BC recruits.

After graduation from advanced training and teaching new recruits, I was ready for a dispatch overseas. In mid-summer, Colonel Davies, my commanding officer, organized a track meet. Each platoon of recruits was ordered to compete. I trained my platoon for the events and was appointed official starter for the sprints. The camp was full of university cadets, all excellent athletes. The members of my platoon were farm boys who could run a mile or two in world class time, but they were oxen as far as a sprint was concerned. To display leadership, which is a burden the officer bears, I disposed of the starter's pistol and entered the 220-yard dash on behalf of my platoon. My opponents in the final heat were the hot shot cadets. I was assigned the inside lane of a circular track, which meant the cadets were in starting blocks ahead of me. Not knowing how fast they were, I took off as if released by a coiled spring. Foolishly, I came in first by a wide margin. Colonel Davies was at the finish line to greet the winner, and I heard him say, "Ah, one of my officers has finally won a race. You are to be the physical training officer and you are taken off the next overseas draft."

Some months later, however, I was able to rectify my error at a meeting of the officers' mess, when I challenged the commanding officer on the use of mess money. That provoked Colonel Davies to release me from my position as physical training officer and place me on the next overseas draft. He came to the CN Railway Station to say farewell and handed me documents dealing with the soldiers in my charge, adding that one was unsealed and I could read it before sealing it. It was an appraisal of my record as a training officer. He gave me a flattering report, except to say I had "a parade square complex."

I had enjoyed training people to run, climb obstacles and get their backsides and heads down behind stumps, logs or the shelter of ditches. I am sure that saved more lives than precision marching. When I enlisted, I understood Canadians would not be marching forward in a close-packed square as did those unfortunate soldiers in the Battle of Waterloo.

I left Chilliwack for Halifax to board the *Ile de France* with some 20,000 other soldiers. The girl, a week or so earlier, had given birth to our first child, and had come to say farewell. I met her some distance from the station. "Do not come to the station platform," I had pleaded. "Our goodbye should be near your home where we courted. If this should be my last view of you I want it to be in familiar surroundings where you can make a new beginning. My thoughts of you waiting for me in a familiar background are important. Please do not say goodbye on a station platform, watching a train disappear that may never return."

In England I was posted to a signals unit at Aldershot, under orders to commence retraining as a signals officer. I protested: "I am an engineer officer and I am fully trained." My commanding officer was a pompous lieutenant colonel from Toronto, a stockbroker when employed. He had no idea how the army could screw up a posting and did not care. I was to become a signals officer and that was the end of the discussion. Six days later I was still managing a one-man rebellion, refusing to attend training classes. The man from Toronto did not know what to do about it.

Two weeks into the entanglement I met Norman McConnell, a Vancouver mining executive and engineer officer, who had trained at Chilliwack and travelled overseas with me. He was posted to Transport and was experienced in mapping and air photographic procedures through his work in mineral exploration. He had seen a notice soliciting applications for posting to an air survey company, so we formulated a plan. Norm arranged an interview. On the appointed day, he was paraded before a major wearing the badge of the First Canadian Air Survey Company, RCE. The major listened to Norm's superb qualifications, but Norm expressed reluctant interest and in a spirit of co-operation told the major that I was the right candidate for the work. I was interviewed immediately. I acknowledged my qualifications and experience and gave a sales pitch detailing Norm's credentials. The major was convinced he had discovered two secret weapons. In short order, he unlocked and aborted the military tangle that had diverted Norm and me to another unnecessary sequence of training.

Norm and I joined the First Canadian Air Survey Company and within days plunged into operations. The company worked two twelve-hour shifts per day producing a map sheet, detailing the coastline of France and examining every potential attack area. We did not work exclusively for Canadian formations since British and American high command adopted BC mapping methodology. In that context we mapped current air photos, which were often photographs only hours old and, on many occasions, taken expressly for our use. This provided a base map on which to overprint in the study of potential battle sectors. These maps included all of the French coast along the English Channel and the Biscay coast inland for five miles. Early in 1944 we concentrated on the Normandy sector and the beach access areas, including the pre–D Day Orne River parachute landing sites. This work was allocated to the Canadian air survey at the request of central command headquarters, of which General Eisenhower was chief.

Thanks to Napoleon Bonaparte, the church spires of France had been meticulously triangulated to establish precise geodetic coordinates and the height of the spires above sea level were recorded. This gave us a grid on which we could fit details to precise scale, including accurate mapping of land forms, buildings, ditches, roads, railways, forest cover and even individual trees. The Napoleonic grid gave 100 percent accuracy, far superior to the uncertainly positioned mountaintops used as the grid in BC air mapping technology.

The company commander, Major L.G. Trorey, had worked in the Victoria Air Survey headquarters established by F.D. Mulholland. Trorey translated and expanded skills learned from Gerry Andrews and Bill Hall, men who had participated in pioneering air surveys with the BC Forest Service, particularly in the 1938 Okanagan Survey.

In June 1943, General McNaughton assigned Lieutenant Colonel Andrews to command Canadian Army Air Survey Liaison, with orders to co-ordinate British, Canadian and American air photographic and survey specifications. Six months later His Majesty's New Year's honours list included the name of G.S. Andrews. He was granted the Most Excellent Order of the British Empire at an investiture at Buckingham Palace on February 15, 1944.

By then it was already D Day for my unit, First Canadian Air Survey. In secret we were well advanced in mapping the coast of France. Operation Overlord had an urgent need for detailed hydrography to determine the underwater formations of the landing beaches. Royal engineers and a Cambridge professor worked out a classic hydrodynamic equation that correlated the velocity of waves approaching the beach with the depth of water. Andrews promptly transposed the formula to air photo interpretation, and we were able to calculate the depth of water on potential landing beaches. Then the race was on to map underwater contours for all the invasion beaches, particularly Juno Beach where the Canadians were to go ashore. In the same period we prepared detailed maps of the Orne River bridges, which was where the British and Canadian paratroopers were to land out of the dawn sky.

While air photography and mapping were pre-war intelligence tools, the science was underdeveloped and not adaptable to mass production technology under battlefield conditions. It was British Columbians who pioneered and expanded military technology for use in sight and sound of the guns and bombs. It was a British Columbian who led the First Canadian Air Survey Company. That we could establish the objective of "a map a day the day needed" and make it work was a singular achievement, much of it shaped by the forest survey technology pioneered in BC.

On the home front, F.D. Mulholland, forester and wounded veteran of World War I, who had fought to establish air survey technology, could smile with pride. In the face of appalling odds caused by the disinterest of Chief Forester Manning and the obstruction of C.D. Orchard, F.D. had obtained an allocation of money for the development of air survey technology. He was well pleased with his boys from the Forest Surveys Division of the BC Forest Service. If Mulholland had been lazy or uncaring, and not so endowed with perseverance, the bureaucracy of government would have defeated him and many Canadian names would have been added to the casualty lists. Wars have unsung heroes; F.D. Mulholland is one.

Andrews, on return from military duty pioneering and co-ordinating air photographic interpretation and intelligence work, was full of ideas to improve forestry procedures in BC. But his great abilities, combined with the fact that he was a protégé of Mulholland, put him on the blacklist of C.D. Orchard, who by war's end was chief forester. Andrews was entitled to employment in his former job at the very least, but he was qualified for a more senior position, many of which were available because of war casualties and resignations. In a petty action, Orchard reassigned Andrews to his previous junior position. George Melrose, the deputy minister of lands, employed Andrews in the surveyor general's office. Very soon Andrews was appointed surveyor general, where he modernized and reshaped land survey procedures in the province and became known as one of the world's greatest innovators of modern technology in the science of surveying. His record of professional and military service to his home province is not widely known. In retirement, in his ninth decade, he continues to contribute to his profession. Like most first and second-generation foresters, he has a deep love of British Columbia.

Shortly after D Day, our survey company, with its significant component of British Columbians, landed on Normandy Beach and moved in close support of the advance eastward to cross the Rhine. In battlefield conditions, using mobile generators to power instruments and photo processing, drafting and printing equipment, we supplied almost instant photographs and maps to forward field commanders. Nothing like this had been done before and our success was tremendous. In about sixteen months of unremitting toil — from late 1943 until the winddown of hostilities — the First Canadian Air Survey Company made 428 maps, all dealing with the advance across Normandy Beach through France, Belgium and Holland, then over the Rhine into Germany. In addition, we made maps for deviations from the path of Canadian troops. We did work for Americans in France, and for the British and Canadians who cleared the Germans from the Walchern Islands to replace the long, slow movement of supplies overland from Normandy and Cherbourg.

At the end of hostilities in Europe, the long wait from VE Day until the troop ship departed from Southampton was an eternity. The job was done and I was going home. Only those who heard the guns go silent and realized the sky was free of bomb-laden aircraft would understand a soldier's thoughts when facing homeward. I was alive and I was going home. I do not think I had wept since age five. On VE Day I wept.

Since I would return to a job in the forest industry and be

involved in producing goods for reconstruction, I had points awarded in the complicated system dreamed up by politicians fearful of mass unemployment among discharged soldiers. My homecoming number came up in September 1945. I was detached from command of my platoon in Germany and went to Southampton to awaited the vessel *Louis Pasteur*, scheduled to leave in twenty-four hours.

There I met another officer being shuttled home to a job. Like me, he had relieved a German officer of American and British money which, in our respective zeal to pack up and go home, ended up in our kit bags. To dispose of the money during the wait for the ship's departure we pooled resources and went to Exeter where we stayed in Judges Lodgings, a lavish hotel where judges of the court rested after their days of toil. We hired a taxi and, with the meter ticking, did a tour of the Devonshire countryside. Once the money was disposed of on food, drink and taxi fares, we boarded ship with empty pockets.

Then came the long, dreary trip across the Atlantic to Quebec City. My first realization that I was home in Canada was on entering the Gulf of St. Lawrence as it narrows. There in the distance was a Canadian train in a cloud of surging steam, its whistle echoing from the hillside. A real train and a real steam whistle, like the ones in BC logging camps, not the thin, tiny bleats of a toy-like European train. It was real, it was Canadian.

In mid-September the Canadian prairie was snow-clad, and my long days of travelling had begun to tell. I was sleepless, actually counting every click of the train wheels on the two ribbons of steel. I telephoned the girl, my wife, and asked her to come east to meet me. At Kamloops we met and spent several days getting reacquainted. Then it was on to Chilliwack. The war ended for me when I disembarked on the same station platform from whence I had begun my service overseas. The girl and I went to the same spot where we had parted, and from there we walked hand in hand to meet my daughter.

The experience of soldiering in France never leaves one, and emerges as a strong emotion from time to time. In about 1973, I had occasion to examine road building equipment in a factory near Paris. Before returning home I rented a car, intent on revisiting the Normandy battlefields. Near Caen, the memories came flooding back. It is wise not to return to battlefields unless they are those of an ancient war in a long forgotten century.

During my service as a soldier in Britain, I spent many of my leaves in Scotland, visiting my mother's relatives. They took me to visit Douglas fir plantations in the highlands near Crainlarich, in the shadow of Ben Nevis. It was here I saw crop-replacing silviculture on the bare hills of Scotland, which had been clear-cut starting in the early 1800s.

In 1987, I visited a Scottish forest I had first seen some forty-four years earlier. It had been planted with Douglas fir seed imported from BC, and harvested for sawlog timber at age forty. Now, in 1987, the second crop was at Christmas tree size. While the girl breakfasted in the hotel at Crainlarich I went across the street to the railway siding to examine fifteen or twenty railcar loads of Douglas fir and Sitka spruce logs, which were larger and of a higher quality than one now sees in common use in BC. I climbed a fence to inspect the logs and count the rings, and learned that the forest was harvested at thirty-eight years of age and the stump diameters exceeded twenty inches. This was superb timber. The forester informed me he had clear-cut and followed with a new plantation. He said the thirty-eight-year growth cycle included two commercial thinnings which had provided additional timber equal to the clear-cut volume.

When I returned from Europe, I went to Ucluelet on the west coast of Vancouver Island. I wanted to examine areas logged by my contracting company twenty-five years earlier, in 1962, on the Tree Farm Licence held for thirty-five years by British Columbia Forest Products Limited. In that period BC Forest Products had succeeded in stripping the flatland on the Ucluelet-Tofino peninsula that once grew cedar and hemlock of a classic quality and volume per acre. I found the land had been planted with Douglas fir on soil not silviculturally appropriate to that species. In addition, the land was so cluttered with debris and weeds that the trees were unhealthy and unlikely ever to mature. In Scotland the trees would have been fifty feet tall and commercial thinnings of usable timber would have been carried out on two occasions. But not in British Columbia. The foresters responsible for this sickly Ucluelet forest, wherever they now are, should hang their heads in shame.

On the same peninsula, on the eastward hills framing Pacific Rim Park, there is a vast expanse, an entire range of mountains, that is one huge clear-cut, its soil exposed to monsoonlike rainfall. Scattered through that clear-cut is abandoned timber — public property wasted — a subsidy to two companies controlled from some location far from BC.

This is not silviculture. This is not "Forests Forever". It is damage inflicted on the people of Tofino and Ucluelet, two once-vibrant communities. It is a theft of public heritage, condoned by a Ministry of Forests that has abandoned every ethic implicit in the Magna Carta responsibility of a forester.

In Ucluelet, I met a former employee, Danny, a native of the Nootka Nation. Danny told me a disturbing story.

In about 1980 MacMillan Bloedel, operating on a Tree Farm Licence in Barkley Sound, was issued a cutting permit by the Forest Service. A trespass occurred on Indian land. The Indians made a claim for payment of damages and requested that new trees suitable to the forest soil be planted. In the opinion of the Indians, cedar, which is a sacred tree in their culture, should have been planted. M & B planted hemlock, most of which died, and the company failed to compensate the natives for the timber removed from their land. M & B alleged that responsibility for the mistake rested with the Ministry of Forests because its cutting plan map failed to record the existence of Indian land. After eight years of talk, five groups of lawyers housed in five highrise buildings were still involved in a battle of words. Two of these towers of frustration housed separate and opposing Vancouver law offices. Another was in Ottawa. One more was home to the Ministry of Forests in Victoria, and the fifth, the largest of all, was M & B's massive highrise fortress. At that point, nothing had been settled.

"My goodness, Danny," I said, "there is only a few thousand dollars' worth of logs and a few acres of new forest to plant. What is the problem?"

He replied, "I think the issue is that the Ministry of Forests says it cannot be held liable for its negligence. It has no accountability."

I came away from Ucluelet saddened by what the land had told me — abuse of the soil, and waste of public property. The waste was due to disregard of public equity by accountable professional foresters in the public employ.

If one can claim to gain anything from a war, I must say that it offered me a chance to see how forestry is practised elsewhere, and gave me a standard to apply when returning to BC. Often my thoughts go back to forests I have either visited, worked in or examined in other parts of the world where there is first class forestry. These places make it clear that British Columbia is on a downward spiral.

With many others, I went through the war as a professional forester, and one of the things I thought I was doing was to protect a country and a system of government that looks after its resources and is responsive to the concerns of its citizens. Today it is clear there are more battles to be fought. In 1945, when we returned from Europe, we thought we had conquered tyranny. In Scotland I had seen how forestry could be practised. I was eager to come home to BC, with its vast, untouched lands, its rich forest soils and climate suited to growing magnificent stands of trees. It seemed, at that point, that a bountiful future lay before us. It took me some time to learn that while we were away at war, that future had been sadly curtailed, to an extent we are only now beginning to understand.

CHAPTER 7

The Birth of the Tree Farm Licence Concept

By 1942, most foresters of my generation were in wartime Europe, in an all-out effort for a victory that seemed remote and uncertain. The Germans had driven the British out of Europe, the Japanese had attacked Pearl Harbor, Hong Kong had fallen to enemy hands, Japanese Canadians had been evacuated from the BC coast. For the Allies, particularly Canada, 1942 was perhaps the blackest period of the war. It was not a time when sustained yield forestry in BC seemed important.

What we knew about events in British Columbia was not encouraging. The political situation there was unstable. In December, 1941, Duff Pattullo's Liberals had lost their majority and the socialist CCF had received one-third of the votes — a startling surge of support. At a raucous convention, the Liberal party voted to elect John Hart as its new leader and to join the Conservatives in a coalition government. The province's forest industry was running flat out, supplying critical materials to the war effort but severely hampered by a shortage of manpower. The Forest Service had been stripped of personnel. The chief forester, E.C. Manning, had been killed in an air crash in

February 1941, and C.D. Orchard had been appointed in his place.

On August 27, just ten days after the Dieppe disaster in Europe, C.D. Orchard delivered to A. Wells Gray, the Minister of Lands, a twenty-five-page discussion paper proposing "sustained yield," together with seven pages of draft legislation. The proposal was titled "Forest Working Circles: An analysis of Forest Legislation in British Columbia as it relates to disposal of Crown timber, and proposed legislation designed to institute managed harvesting on the basis of perpetual yield."

Orchard later appended a note to his personal copy of the memorandum:

> This memorandum was prepared and submitted to the Minister of Lands, the Honourable A. Wells Gray, August 1942.... Mr. Gray read it, discussed it with me, and took it to the Premier, Hon. John Hart, who kept it for more than a year, discussing it with me and with his friends in the industry, some of whom he sent to me to argue the matter and then report back to him.... There were about a dozen copies.
>
> In December 1943 the premier, Mr. Hart, called me to his office, when he told me that the government was "sold" on my proposals, but could not hope to get such a radical change of policy through the legislature if it were introduced "cold." He, therefore, proposed to appoint a royal commission, he thought one man and hoped it would be Chief Justice, Hon. Gordon Sloan to canvas the proposition both for the value of his finding and a measure of public education.... Sloan was appointed accordingly as of 31 December, 1943. In the meantime Mr. Gray died. For some time the premier, Mr. Hart, was acting minister of Lands.

Later, in his memoirs, Orchard described his relationship

with the minister for whom he prepared his historic memorandum:

> Mr. Gray was a gentle man (gentleman too) and a politician. He had been for seventeen years mayor of New Westminster; had never been defeated in an election, was a friend of everybody, and Scotch whiskey. An easy touch for all the bums he encountered. I was told he often arrived home in New Westminster without a coat, hat and even shoes. He was my delight and my despair. He went home to New Westminster frequently. Friday pm his secretary would come to my office with a request to get the minister a bottle or two for the trip. Until I evolved a solution getting that bottle meant abandoning whatever one had been doing for a half-hour visit to the liquor store in the middle of a work a day afternoon. Shortly I was picking up the Minister's bottles at some convenient passing of the store, caching them at my desk at the office. Thereafter I was able to give fast service without interfering with work or the risk of public stigma.

There are several aspects of Orchard's actions at this time that bear examination if the evolution of provincial forest policy is to be understood. In the first place, the new chief forester was not the non-partisan civil servant that he describes himself to be in his memoirs. In fact, he was an active Liberal, who at a later date almost ran as a Liberal candidate in a provincial election. While this devotion to the Liberal cause may not have influenced what he wrote in the memo to Wells Gray, it was certainly a factor in the events touched off by the memo.

In addition, the circumstances in which the memo was prepared, presented and dealt with are worth noting. The attention and energy of virtually everyone in BC were, at this time, devoted to winning a war that appeared to be lost. It was a curious time to be drafting and implementing a major shift in provincial forest policy, when many of the most knowledgeable professionals and others whose advice would be helpful were otherwise engaged.

It is interesting to speculate on John Hart's discussions with select industrial leaders. At this period, one of his major objectives was to obtain financial support for the Liberals so the Conservatives could be dumped from the coalition. It would be naïve to assume that party financing and future forest tenure opportunity were not discussed in the same breath.

Robert Filberg of the Canadian Western Lumber Company gave support, and was later successful in getting commitments for the first two Forest Management Licences (later changed to Tree Farm Licences) allocated. Officials of the Powell River Company, known to be financial supporters of the Liberal-controlled coalition government, participated. H.R. MacMillan, perhaps the only industrialist whose experience as a professional forester qualified him to express an opinion, was not contacted.

In his memo to Premier John Hart, Orchard made the doom and gloom prediction that the supply of mature timber in the province would last only thirty-three years unless a sustained yield management policy was implemented immediately. Forest inventory data from surveys carried out in the decade before the war was available to him, but Orchard told a vastly different story, quoting estimates made in 1936 before the air survey program was launched.

> In 1912 we believed that we had, perhaps did have, 300 billion feet of merchantable timber, which we were then harvesting at the rate of about ¼ billion feet per year. Making no allowance for annual growth (of trees) it would take (the industry) nearly 250 years to use up merely the mature timber now standing. In 1941, following cutting and twenty years of intensive surveys

and collection and tabulation of data designed to give us accurate knowledge, we estimate a capital stock of 110 billion feet of accessible merchantable timber, which we are cutting at the rate of ⅓ billion board feet per year. After a lapse of a short twenty-nine years our visible resources have shrunk from 250 years' supply to 33 years.

Orchard pointed out, quite correctly, that there were three fundamental problems for which solutions must be found if deterioration of the forest resource was to be halted. Solutions included providing adequate fire protection, ensuring that every acre deforested was under crop again with least possible delay and limiting the cut to the productive capacity of the new forest.

Orchard then reviewed legislation, and found that the existing policy of public land ownership and competitive timber sales no longer worked.

Its weakness rests on the fact that it forces the licencee or operator into a position where he has no personal interest whatever other than removing from the land as quickly as possible all existing values. Inevitably he will do this in such a manner as to make the greatest possible profit. So far as the operator is concerned, it is a system of "cut out and get out," of "timber mining" deliberately imposed by strictly enforced law.

To this point, apart from his estimates of timber supply remaining in the province, Orchard's description of the state of forest administration in BC was fairly accurate and widely understood. His numbers, and much of his description, had come right from F.D. Mulholland's inventory report, *The Forest Resources of British Columbia*, published four years earlier from data gathered by the survey crews I worked for as a student.

Orchard's policy solution, the imposition of perpetual or sustained yield management, was a well-known theory of forestry that had been discussed for decades, ever since it was introduced in North America around the start of the nineteenth century. Essentially, sustained yield theory said that the annual harvest in a defined forest area (called a "working circle" by Orchard) should equal the volume of timber grown in the rest of that forest during that year. If the forest had an even distribution of age classes, the theory went, it could be harvested at that level forever.

But there were problems in applying sustained yield theory to BC forests. The first was that there was not an even distribution of age classes—the entire uncut forest was classed as "mature" and ranged from a few years to many centuries in age. This made it difficult to determine how fast to cut the mature forest in the sustained yield unit, or working circle, so that the annual harvest could be maintained. Without accurate inventory and growth figures, it was impossible to set an accurate annual allowable cut.

Even if this problem could be overcome, Orchard was still faced with the problem of how to persuade anyone—the government had already demonstrated that it was unwilling—to limit their annual harvest, to ensure the cutover lands were restocked and the new forests tended until they were the right age for harvesting. In most of the rest of the world, managed forests were already-defined and relatively small tracts of privately owned land; BC had yet to find a tenure mechanism that provided the incentive to make sustained yield possible. Orchard argued:

> It is submitted here that the rational solution is to give the operator, wherever possible, an interest in the area he is working that will permit him to make long term plans in co-operation with government, and permit him to see the possibility at some later date of retrieving

capital invested and profits delayed in the immediate
interest of forest conservation. This proposal is made in
the belief that private interest can be made to coincide
with public interest and that private interest can be
substituted for penalties and coercion.

Adoption of this principle would involve the pooling
of private and crown forest land in sufficient area to
support in perpetuity, if managed in accordance with
sound forest practice, the industrial unit it is desired to
stabilize . . .

The primary objective would be to secure perpetual
and uninterrupted yield for our forest lands, stabilize
existing industries which have already made themselves
fundamental factors in the economic life of the province,
to preserve for the continued use of the Province investments, management, experience and employment, and
to prevent the economic waste involved in establishing
new forest industries, some of which are proposed on a
short-term basis when they might, with a little more
foresight, be made perpetual.

Orchard's major error concerned the motivation of loggers,
whom he accused, then and with greater emphasis later, of
wanting only to "cut and get out." At this time, the only forms
of tenure available on public land prohibited the loggers from
doing anything more than logging and leaving. Many loggers,
and I have met scores of them in the coastal communities,
would have liked very much to practise sustained yield on a plot
of land, had they been allowed to acquire it. In a timber sale it
was not a part of their agreement with the Crown to reforest
and tend future crops. Government reserved this responsibility
for itself but did nothing to carry it out except squander the
timber sale income that was available for reforestation. That
this vital step in sustained yield was not being carried out was
a failure of the Forest Service, of which Orchard was the head,

or of the government, to which he was the chief forest adviser. Blaming the logger was silly, and it would lead Orchard to commit some major errors in administering the reshaped forest policies that eventually resulted from his memo.

Visible in Orchard's proposal are his particular prejudices. He opposed private ownership of forests and forest land. He sought administrative control of all forest land in the province. His memoirs reveal a profound dislike of the McBride era lease and a yearning to control these "offensive tenures." He criticized actions of major companies owning private forests in the E & N Belt. In 1936, in the agony of a depressed economy, some of them had implemented reforestation procedures, in spite of the absence of sensible tax laws at either the federal or provincial level. Orchard, for all his dedication to forestry, had an undisguised and passionate opposition to ownership of forest property by private citizens and corporations; therefore, he was prejudiced against private forestry wherever it existed.

At that time there were many informed and experienced men who believed that since private forest management worked elsewhere, it would work in BC. Orchard discussed the Tree Farm Licence scheme with one of these men — S.G. Smith, manager of Bloedel, Stewart & Welch and one of the most experienced and responsible loggers on the Pacific coast. Orchard wrote:

> Mr. Smith apparently agreed that our forest laws and policies were due for an overhaul, but he was less than enthusiastic about my "Management Licences." He proposed that we should give holders of renewable special timber licences, lease, and like tenures, which now only conferred the right to remove timber, the right to acquire outright ownership. In other words, abandon the long-established policy of public ownership of land in favour of private ownership favoured in the United States and the Maritime provinces. I couldn't see any

possibility of such a policy gaining approval in BC and in any event I don't approve. So far, any private owner- ship that I had observed certainly had not tended to promote conservative forest use in America.

Orchard was certainly wrong in his assessment that private forestry did not function well in America. In Orchard's time, private US owners had created the largest man-made forest in the world, some 90 million acres in the former cotton belt. During the same period in BC, in the E & N Belt, less than two hours from Orchard's office, sustained crop replacement on private land ranked as world class and greatly exceeded the quality of crop replacement on public land in Orchard's juris- diction. Opposition to private ownership of forest land was simply a phobia of Orchard's. His statement that it would never gain approval in BC is an old argument used by people who do not like private property ownership.

While Orchard had a vision of sustained yield, he also had some serious handicaps. He did not understand the silvicul- tural requirements for BC's species, climate and land form. His background and experience were in bureaucracy and adminis- tration. He knew next to nothing about BC's forests and never showed an interest in the natural, biological processes that are the basis of forest management. Nor did he know much about the harvesting end of the forest business: he seemed to view loggers as a necessary evil. Compounding this mistake was the fact that Forest Service officials had grown used to the domi- nance of railway logging: Orchard's program was founded on the expectation that railway logging would continue.

Orchard also had a confused, even simplistic grasp of eco- nomics. His ignorance in this area led him to propose a tenure system that was distorted and eventually corrupted because of a capital gains law that gave away billions of dollars in public equity. Orchard did not know about this factor until it was too late. He thought forestry existed apart from business and economics, and that the activity of growing trees as a crop was a branch of engineering. He never did understand that silviculture is a business, an error that has infected the Forest Service ever since.

Orchard was naïve in respect to tax laws as they affected silviculture. He did not know the federal Income Tax Act and the provincial Land Tax Act were compelling barriers to crop-replacing silviculture on lands owned or controlled by corporations or private citizens. The federal law disallowed the cost of silviculture in any form as an expense against income earned, which is like telling a prairie farmer that what he spent buying seed and plowing his land was not to be deducted from the selling price of wheat. Exacerbating the situation, provincial authorities classed denuded, privately owned forest land as "wild land" and assessed it at a tax rate six times the rate applied to all other crop land.

The Sloan Royal Commission sat through 1944, with Orchard serving as chief aide and adviser. One person to appear before Sloan was MacMillan, who came from wartime service in Ottawa to offer his views. He supported the idea of sustained yield forest management, but had some reservations about its implementation.

Macmillan voiced a warning that inept forest administration could well be the rock on which Orchard's concept would founder.

> It is admitted that there can be no orderly management of British Columbia forests to attain annual crops in perpetuity until it is possible to produce working plans. It should therefore be made clear there are probably not five foresters in British Columbia who have ever seen a working plan. Furthermore, a dependable working plan cannot be produced without classification of the site qualities of the area for which the plan is required, together with ample knowledge of growth

rates and the silvicultural habits of the tree species on the respective sites. To accumulate such facts requires years of field work by trained foresters, which has not yet been started.

Once, many years later, when I asked him about his appearance at the commission, he said: "I intended it as a warning that just putting words expressing a theory into a statute was no guarantee of a solution." He went on to say that implementation would depend on strong, determined leadership by competent men who were prepared to speak out against the abuse of the forest by industry and to oppose political interference, because nothing could be worse than having to depend on the ebb and flow of political will for financial and other support to forest preservation.

When he spoke to the commission, MacMillan did not predict that the political system would feed off Orchard's management tenure in the outrageous fashion in which it eventually did. With a long career as a responsible civil servant and business executive, he could not imagine such an outrage.

In one of my last conversations with MacMillan in the late 1950s, we discussed how far Orchard's concept, as modified by Sloan in his first royal commission report, had been pulled off course. MacMillan said that Orchard had had a noble purpose, he believed in sustained yield forestry and he took on the burden of implementation. Few in Canada have had the temerity to accept such a challenge. But Orchard's concept was overwhelmed by his inadequate knowledge of the provincial forest and the essentials of silviculture. Thereafter, he was defeated by raw politics and the people of BC are the victims.

It is prophetic that in 1945 H.R. MacMillan warned Chief Justice Sloan and members of the forestry profession:

Logging has been going on for decades but foresters have displayed neither the curiosity nor the ambition to

collect and publish elementary growth studies as could
have been got together with minimum of expense and
effort. . . . The fact that the present crop of commercial
timber will sustain the forest industry on its present scale
for another two generations or so should not lull us to
sleep. It is still as necessary as ever to provide the next
crop. Barely enough time remains to do it. We can afford
no more losses of either immature forest by fire or of
existing crop by skimming off only the cream when
reaping it.

Speaking to government, through Sloan, MacMillan said:

In nature the old forest produces the new forest. In
public finance the revenue from liquidation of the old
forest must be used to the degree necessary to produce
the new forest. It is community suicide in the coastal
forest district to expect the mature forest to employ the
people, supply the revenue for building roads and public
works, produce the money for education and defence
systems, carry social services and full employment and
at the same time reproduce itself automatically without
expense.

CHAPTER 8

The Great Debate

On my return to Vancouver in September 1945, the Sloan
Royal Commission hearings were finished, but the report
was not yet written. Every forester I talked to was convinced a
new age of forestry was upon us and sustained yield management would soon be a reality.

I enjoyed an all-too-brief visit with my parents. Two of my
brothers were soon to be discharged from the air force, one as
a pilot, the other as a navigator. The third brother was a tank
corps gunner who had landed on D Day and who, after VE Day,
had been assigned to serve in the army of occupation in Germany. My sister was attached to a US Army unit in Alaska.
My mother and father were happy: five of their children in
military service were safe and sound. But they were concerned
about the availability of jobs, as unemployment lines length-
ened when the troops came home.

I had a job waiting in the plywood industry, under the
guarantee to servicemen that their pre-service employment
would remain available to them. I visited Jimmy Jones, the

99

personnel manager at Fraser Mills, and signed a paper certifying that I had voluntarily waived my right to my old job. This formality freed me to search for opportunities in forestry. Uppermost in my mind was work in silviculture. In Scotland, I had examined sparkling plantations of Douglas fir and Sitka spruce grown from seed collected in BC. In eastern France, vibrant pine plantations that had survived the war added beauty and serenity to the land. In Germany, just before we crossed the Rhine, we fought along the roadways while above us, on the hillsides, there stood a thirty-year-old Douglas fir forest, grown from seed collected on Vancouver Island. The German trees were large enough to use for pilings; the Canadian Forestry Corps had harvested them to stabilize the mud banks of canals and the area surrounding Bailey bridge sites.

I took a job with a small sawmill company in New Westminster that specialized in cutting alder. They were looking for a log supply in the Squamish Valley and I accepted employment as their log buyer and forester, commissioned to seek out land suitable for growing an alder crop. One reason I was persuaded to accept the job was that a car was to be supplied. In those days, cars were rationed and a long, long wait faced the purchaser. Used car prices were theoretically pegged under the price control law, but the actual black market price was nearly as high as that of a new car. On accepting employment I offered to purchase the car for $450, which was the price control value, although my employer had paid nearly $1,000 for it. I was twenty-nine years of age, married with one child and this was the first car I ever owned. It was a treasure.

The job was short-lived, however. My employer lost interest in manufacturing alder lumber and I was put to work as a log buyer, wandering the log storage grounds of the Fraser River and negotiating the purchase of hemlock. I was about as far from the forest as I could be, so I resigned.

At the request of C.J. Haddon, one of the few people without a forestry degree to be appointed district forester, I joined the

Forest Service as a manager of timber sales in the Vancouver Forest District. A few months into the job, I was assigned the task of helping a Vancouver Island ranger deal with a dispute with Gordon Gibson at his logging show near Jeune Landing.

Gibson was in the embarrassing position of having trespassed on land outside his licence area. The ranger had made an estimate of the volume of wood cut in the trespass and removed without scaling, but he was having a hard time dealing with Gibson. Gibson, in his "bull of the woods" manner, argued loudly that the volume was grossly overestimated and that the stumpage charged for it was outrageously high.

The ranger and I went unannounced to Jeune Landing and began measuring stumps. Before long Gibson arrived.

"Young man," he demanded, "what are you doing in my timber sale?"

"I have measured out the trespass acreage," was my response, "and I am now counting and measuring all the stumps. I will apply tree height factors and that will confirm the timber volume on which you owe money."

"But that's not fair," he roared at me.

I carried on with my work and for the rest of that day and part of the next, he tagged along, grumbling about the presence of someone from the Vancouver office, when he wanted to deal directly with the ranger.

When I was finished, he asked, "How much do I owe you?"

"I'll calculate it and send you an invoice," I replied. "But just as an estimate, the trespass fine is equal to about three years of my salary, so I've had a couple of days of good work." As he looked none too pleased with this information, I couldn't resist adding, "Mr. Gibson, you know you are not supposed to trespass and I would appreciate that if it ever happens again you will respect the duty of the ranger to do his job to report and scale it. Next time please don't hassle him."

Gibson looked a little shocked at this and I thought he was going to erupt again. But instead he burst out laughing. "Young fellow, you have done your job and I like people who do that. How about coming to work for me?"

I declined with thanks, explaining that I wanted experience in forestry. In spite of his bluster, then and in the years that followed, I always found Gibson to be one of the most genuine and kind-hearted men I ever met.

When I returned to my office in the Marine Building I found the staff celebrating an across-the-board pay increase just announced by the Civil Service Commission. But my next paycheque was written for the old amount. Perplexed, I went to see Haddon, who told me my increase had been denied because I had been hired at a higher salary than others with more seniority, and that the Victoria office had turned down my raise in spite of his protest. The next day I submitted my resignation and took a timber cruising job mapping topography at Vancouver Bay in Jervis Inlet.

At about this time, quite by accident, I encountered F.D. Mulholland. He had left the Forest Service to become chief forester of Canadian Western Lumber Company, making him one of the first industrial foresters of his generation. As Mulholland had been my mentor in my pre-war Forest Service survey work,he asked me what I had been doing since then. I brought him up to date and asked him his views on sustained yield and the likely recommendations of the Sloan Commission.

"The way the Sloan Royal Commission has been conducted," Mulholland said, "it is doubtful that the new forest legislation will allow individual citizens access to land to participate in the business of growing trees as a crop."

F.D. predicted that demands on the publicly owned forest were likely to increase. The Forest Service had no plan and much less intent to practise silviculture in supplying a new crop. A new crop would find a ready market when the virgin crop was gone. The new crop was also essential for the future prosperity of a non-agricultural region such as the coast of

British Columbia. Study of land ownership in forest-oriented European countries had confirmed that private ownership of land could create successful tree farmers. There was a host of potential tree farmers among fishermen and forest industry workers who were seasonally employed and living in the small communities of coastal BC. "These people," he said, "more than city folk, have a stake in forestry and they must be allowed to have access to land."

It was the remote communities, said Mulholland, that needed the assurance of sustained yield forest management and, hence, jobs for their residents. They needed to know that their investment in their community would remain viable. "Foresters should be careful," he said, "not to create ghost towns."

Then Mulholland all but roared. "Orchard's priority is all wrong. The big companies will get all the timber and the ordinary working man will get the runaround. The forest management licence scheme is too one-sided and it will be fiddled out of shape by a bunch of uncaring bureaucrats taking orders from a forest dictator in the person of a chief forester. This is not wanted in Canada."

Mulholland went on to say that the merits of a strong core of land-owning tree farmers had not been well articulated to the royal commission. He volunteered to mail me copies of discussion papers that dealt with the issue.

He kept his promise, and sent me a copy of a speech he had made to the Canadian Society of Forest Engineers in December 1939, titled "Forest Policy: Ownership and administration lessons from other countries." Some time later, he mailed me a copy of a speech Orchard had given in Regina, titled "The functions of the State in the management of Crown and private forests for the production of an assured supply of wood for industry."

These two speeches contain the substance of a great debate over the relative merits of public and private ownership and management of forests. Largely because of Orchard's determined opposition, the option of placing a portion of BC's forest land in private hands was not seriously considered by Sloan. But in the period between the end of the commission hearings and the release of the revised Forest Act based on Sloan's report, Mulholland was keeping the debate alive.

Orchard had long been at odds with the former head of forest surveys. Mulholland persisted in championing the outstanding success of private forest management in Europe, and stating his view that the "mess" in Canada was because public administration of forests was in the hands of professional foresters unwilling or unable to perform viable forest management.

In his speech to the engineers, Mulholland presented some figures on the ownership of forest land in several other countries. In Sweden, Finland and Norway, between 60 and 80 percent of forestland was in private ownership, in contrast to 8 percent of privately owned forest in Canada, and less than 4 percent in BC.

Mulholland went on to detail his argument. While almost 80 percent of forest land was privately owned in Sweden, there were relatively few large estates. Only 7 percent of the area classified as farm was in that category. The average farm forest had 75 acres. Finland, meanwhile, encouraged small owners with favourable tax laws and technical assistance. While European countries recognized the national interest in the maintenance of production on forest land, there were basic laws against devastation by private owners; the state commonly concerned itself only with management of public forests.

In Sweden, private forestry was controlled, and the state law was administered by local boards of three members appointed by owners, county council and government. The cost of administration was paid by the participating land owners.

In Germany, restrictions on private forestry, imposed by the various state governments, ranged all the way from complete freedom to enforcement of management plans approved by the state. Moreover, a considerable proportion of private lands was in use, which meant the owner had a life interest only in the income. He could not sell or deplete the property. There was in the German consciousness a belief in the sanctity of this land, dating from the early ages. The land was different from any other kind of property; it was ownership in trust. This concept was reflected in laws prohibiting the break-up of farms, with their forest land, by sale or divided inheritance. Mulholland told the engineers:

> It is reasonable to conclude, from the experience of these countries, that British Columbia would be well advised to adjust its forest policy so as to encourage private forestry. The nature of forest administration which has been successful in European democracies should be observed. Their principles have been decentralization and co-operation of independent authorities, in definite contradiction to state coercion. Even the enforcement of the basic forest law concerning private owners has been delegated in the best organized states to associations of the owners themselves.

Orchard answered Mulholland:

> I suggest that, with the single exception of the United States, these proportions [of private ownership] are the result of almost pure chance and circumstances arising out of a long history, most of which antedates any planned forest management. With the advent of the science of forestry countries have accepted ownership conditions as they found them and have sought, as we seek now, to evolve the best plan applicable to their own set of conditions. Out of their experience we can conclude that a half and half basis is a perfectly workable distribution of ownership. . . .
>
> It is my own opinion that government is best able to

own and manage forest lands for timber production. However, a reasonable measure of private ownership and management, ranging up to, but not exceeding fifty percent, and preferably less than fifty percent, would introduce a healthy competition and act as a desirable tonic on management policy and progress. Canada, which retains ninety-two percent of forest lands in public ownership, is in a highly favourable position to evolve policy in this regard, and there should be no hasty nor ill-considered move to alienate the public interest.

. . . It may further be concluded from experience that large forest areas in government control are essential as a balancing factor in any sustained yield management program. This [is what has happened] in the USA. Suffering perhaps from excess democracy the United States for years followed a deliberate policy of disposing of all public interest in natural resources to private ownership. This policy extended to forests to the point where the government was practically eliminated as an owner . . . accordingly United States authorities finally decided unrelieved private ownership cannot be relied upon. It may be assumed from experience that successful forest management nation wide demands a large measure of government ownership and there seems to be no good reason why exclusive government ownership and management of forest lands should not be successful and satisfactory.

In my discussions with Mulholland, he had pointed out that democratic countries allow and encourage individual citizens to own land and grow tree crops for sale to industrial users. "Just as prairie wheat farmers and successor sons grow wheat and sell it to a flour mill," Mulholland said, "a family tree farm enterprise is a strong component in the forest economy in Europe and in the US southern pine region, where abused cotton lands are being converted to forest crops by private investment in tree farming." In his typical outspoken impatience, he had said, "Thus the fundamental policy of permanent forestry is already proven and established. We do not need to debate on that point — merely carry it out, and therein lies the difficulty. We are making no progress, we are blindsiding democratic rights of the citizens and denying British Columbia assured progress in forest management." In sharp disagreement with Orchard, he said, "It is results we want, not political and philosophical ideals on land ownership. Does state ownership work as well [as private ownership]? We have public ownership in British Columbia; the debate should be is it working as well here as private ownership or a mixture of both might do?"

Orchard stated his position in his presentation to Sloan in January 1945:

> It might be argued theoretically that it is the function of the forester to grow the forest crop and that there his interest comes to an end; that harvesting and land tenure need not concern him.
>
> Practically, these three fundamentals — land tenure, forest culture, and harvesting — cannot be divorced. You can afford to harvest forest crops from lands held under a one or five or ten-year tenure, but you cannot afford to grow overlapping crops that will take from 50 to 150 years to mature on lands held under anything less than some form of perpetual tenure.
>
> How forest lands shall be held, who shall own them, who is to harvest the crop, and how the crop is to be harvested, therefore, are questions of primary importance in any intelligent forest program.

Orchard's conclusion was that "the policy of public ownership of forest lands which has obtained in British Columbia up to the present is wise and should be continued." His recommendations on tenure essentially described the working circles that ultimately became Tree Farm Licences, with the important provision that the Crown retain land ownership, leasing land to the private sector.

In his report, Chief Justice Sloan made reference to the ownership debate: "The Licence area is a Tree Farm; who owns it, who manages it, now or in the future, is of secondary importance, provided it is managed with ability, interest, and imagination." In keeping with the decision that Orchard and the Hart government had already made, Sloan came to the untried conclusion that the kind of long-term dedication apparent in private forestry in Europe and the US would also develop on public forest land leased to private corporations under Tree Farm Licences.

It is likely Sloan did not foresee that the leases would be taken over by large, internationally controlled companies with no national roots, no cultural heritage and no Magna Carta forest ethic.

In observing more than forty-two years of Tree Farm Licence operations, I have deduced that the quality of forest crop replacement on this public land is a very thin shadow of private forest land management throughout the world. The comparison can be made without even leaving the province: private forest lands managed by the same companies that have Tree Farm Licences are much better managed than the public lands they lease. It is abundantly clear that the Tree Farm Licence system, devised as means of maintaining government control over the forests, has failed as a way of establishing silviculture and sustaining the yield from BC's forests. Not only is the timber supply declining but the value of the timber we are getting is falling. We are not developing a vibrant, diversified manufacturing sector, but are concentrating more and more of our production into capital-intensive pulp mills that employ fewer and fewer people. There are few people working full-time on the new timber crop in our forests. If the Tree Farm Licence system was working, we would have tens of thousands of people at work in the forests. We would be producing a supply of high-quality logs, which would feed a variety of conversion plants, which would employ thousands of workers throughout the province. We would not be looking at the future of our forests with fear and uncertainty, but with confidence.

What we must do now is take up the great debate that was put on hold more than forty years ago. We must take another look at the effects of Orchard's actions, and at the wise advice of Mulholland that was ignored.

CHAPTER 9

Politicians Take Charge

After working at several jobs, I had flushed the war out of my system, and I set out to obtain employment that would reward me for having pioneered a degree in commerce and forestry. J.V. Fisher, deputy minister of finance in Victoria, was advertising for a professional forester with training in economics so I arranged a meeting with him.

Fisher, in a precise, clipped Oxford University accent, told me one of his tasks was to borrow money for government needs in the New York market. He explained that for BC the terms of these loans, including rates of interest, were based on the reserve of mature timber in public ownership and the government's projected annual cash income from timber sales and tax generation.

Fisher was normally a disciplined, professional executive with a kindly demeanour, but on this occasion he became agitated. His voice moved several notes up the scale and the odd expletive slipped out. "Our chief forester," he explained, "is postulating that only thirty-three years' supply of merchantable

timber remains in public ownership. He is signalling the curtailment of timber sales." Then he exploded. "Orchard is going
to allocate public property on a profit-sharing basis. Industry
profits rise and fall, which means revenue to the public treasury
will be volatile and uncertain. Moreover, he is talking about a
huge curtailment of public revenue."

Fisher muttered to himself and reached for a piece of paper.
He began reading from Orchard's 1942 memorandum to John
Hart, which had been the starting point of the Sloan Royal
Commission report of 1947. "All existing provincial government dues, including taxes, rentals, royalty and stumpage will
cease to apply to the lands included in the working circle, and
in lieu thereof the company shall pay to the government a
nominal annual token rental for the lands, plus an equitable
share of income on a scale to be determined." Fisher looked
squarely at me. "I cannot take a piece of paper like that and
borrow public money," he said. "All taxes eliminated? How do
we function as a province that must borrow money?

"I collect taxes on private land based on timber content,"
Fisher went on. "I rely on the annual income from sales of public
timber. I am going to lose revenue and the people in New York
will raise interest rates and shorten my term of borrowing,
particularly when you people in forestry advertise there is a
timber famine in this province. Only thirty-three years remaining? That must be a distortion. What do you say?"

"I have worked on three major forest surveys," I replied. "The
data revealed a trend of seven or eight times the previous timber
supply estimate. The mature timber volume will last more like
ninety-nine years. I don't think you need to worry. The Americans, in particular, know more about our reservoir of mature
timber than our own Forest Service."

Fisher almost growled. "I have jurisdiction over land and
property taxes and we have been taxing private timber ownerships for many years. I am not going to allow the Forest Service
to legislate my tax base away and leave me to be fettered by the

men in New York. We will have to impose a specific profit tax on logging. I must have a section in my Land Taxation Act that defines assessment procedures and tax rates on private lands." Watching me carefully, he asked, "What can you do for me?"

I knew he wanted a concise reply. "The procedures in Scandinavia base land taxation on the annual growth rate of the forest crop," I said. "If there is a hundred cubic feet of new crop growth per acre-year, the tax assessment is based accordingly. If the yield is only fifty cubic feet the tax would be half as much. It is a concept used widely in capital valuation of land, particularly in agriculture." Fisher allowed himself a tiny smile as I hastened to elaborate. "I can do that for you."

"What about a profit tax on logging?" he asked.

I said I thought it was basically a bookkeeping problem, but the difficulty would be in determining the value of the logs and, with that, the income attributable to logging. I was sure, however, that rules could be worked out.

Effective January 1, 1948, I was appointed timber land appraiser in the Department of Finance. I began by researching land taxation, particularly the Scandinavian system. I consulted tax advisers to government in BC and Ottawa and visited people in industry, including F.D. Mulholland and Sid Smith, my former mentor at Bloedel, Stewart & Welch. Then I wrote the forest land taxation statute for BC that remains in effect to this day. Its content and concept have been copied widely in other forest jurisdictions, notably in the US timber-producing states where world class silvicultural crop replacement is accomplished on privately owned lands.

Orchard was furious from the outset. He appealed to the new minister of lands and forests, E.T. Kenney, demanding that other government departments be denied the right to employ foresters. I went to a meeting attended by Kenney, Fisher and Orchard, and Orchard demanded that the power to tax forests and forest land be taken from the Ministry of Finance and given to Forestry. Fisher, in his precise English, laid out for Kenney just who ran the finances of government, explained that Orchard was simply out of line and indicated the discussion was over. Kenney picked up a file from his desk and began thumbing through it. Fisher left with a polite bow. Orchard and I remained, sitting side by side in silence. I excused myself and left. As I closed the door, Orchard was raging that he had not been supported by the minister of lands and forests.

Next, Orchard approached the Civil Service Commission, alleging that my appointment as a "forester" was in conflict with a policy that granted the title only to men of long service. He argued that my salary exceeded that paid to men who were older and who had served longer. Fortunately for me, Fisher was chairman of the Civil Service Commission. When Orchard and I appeared before a hearing of the Commission, chaired by Fisher, the meeting lasted all of three minutes and the ruling was instant. Orchard went away empty-handed.

But Orchard's campaign continued. As an experienced timber cruiser and commercial evaluator, I found weekend work evaluating forest land for real estate agents in the Victoria area. Soon I noticed my weekend work was being monitored by F.S. MacKinnon, a senior forester in Orchard's office, and not long after that, Fisher received a complaint that I was "moonlighting" and "abusing" my civil service position. Another meeting was called. Orchard and MacKinnon attended and produced photographs of me stepping out of my car, dressed in timber cruiser garb.

Fisher examined the pictures, nodded appreciatively and said, "Excellent! Mr. Mahood is performing commercial land evaluations as an appraiser. He is involved in the marketplace. I must assume his evaluations done for his employer, the tax office of the provincial Ministry of Finance, are equally knowledgeable. I can add that as an employer, I am most pleased with the professional conduct of Mr. Mahood." The Oxford accent added emphasis to the word "professional." I was the first to leave that meeting. Orchard and MacKinnon either capitulated or were ordered to drop the matter. For the entire remainder of his term in office, Orchard shunned Fisher and regarded him as an obstacle to his own peculiar vision of "forest management."

For three and a half years, ending in mid-1951, I organized and administered a tree farm tax system for privately owned forest land in BC. I was sent by my employer to attend discussions on forest taxation in Washington, D.C. and the US southern pine region, for the purpose of informing our tax authorities and, hence, reassuring the BC government's institutional lenders that taxes were indeed assessed on private timber lands. Ironically, the procedure for taxing privately owned forest land, designed in BC, was applied to privately owned lands in the US. These areas have evolved into the largest man-made forest in the world. Lands that were once abused by heavy cotton growing are now pine forests.

By the time I went to work in Victoria, Orchard's Tree Farm Licence scheme was already running off the rails, securely in the hands of Liberal politicians in their desperate bid to stay in power. Again, the evidence can be found in Orchard's papers. His original plan, described in the memo to Hart, had been run past the public during the Sloan Commission hearings. In modified form it found its way into Sloan's report, and then into legislation revising the Forest Act that was passed on April 3, 1947. But long before that date, the government was promising Tree Farm Licences in back room negotiations. Orchard, writing twelve years later from notes made in his office diaries, explains:

Wednesday 22 January 1947 — Celanese interests in the minister's office re timber reserves for a new pulpmill on the islands and adjacent mainland for the support of a mill at Duncan Bay, and under the provisions of the proposed new legislation. [This, eventually was awarded, in modified form, to Comox Logging Company,

Celanese having decided to proceed entirely under their own steam and having secured Management Licence No. 1 as Columbia Cellulose, on the Skeena and Nass, for the support of their new mill at Port Edwards.] At this meeting there were present, Bob Filberg, Geo. Schneider of Celanese from New York, G. Richards from N.Y., and Axel Brandstrom, their forester consultant.

At the time of this meeting the Forest Service already was working on the "Port Edwards" deal; and this was a new proposal to join forces with Comox Logging, a proposal of which we had heard nothing to the time of this meeting. I refused to recommend to the Minister a reserve on fifteen minutes notice, much to the annoyance of Mr. Schneider who said Celanese didn't have to go asking favours — they were too big — they would be more than welcome in Mexico — and more of the same tenor — none of which bothered either the minister, or myself, very much.

This one passage reveals the violated state of Orchard's plan, even before it was legislated into existence some two months later. Orchard's objective had been to combine public land with private land and land held under the turn-of-the-century McBride timber leases, into a working circle or Tree Farm Licence that would be acquired by an existing company to provide a sustained yield of timber. At the time of this meeting the Port Edwards deal had already been struck; what was left unsaid was that Port Edwards, near Prince Rupert, was in new Forest Minister E. T. Kenney's riding. Also missing here is the fact that the ultimate size of public land issued under the scheme was 6.7 million acres — the size of Vermont — and not one acre of the private lands or a McBride lease was included. This was a far larger area than anyone had imagined when the idea was discussed. More to the point, it totally ignored Orchard's first priority in his forest management scheme — to repatriate control of alienated forest, particularly the McBride leases.

The Port Edwards deal was in direct conflict with another of Orchard's chief objectives, to "stabilize existing industries which have already made themselves fundamental factors in the economic life of the province, to preserve the continued use of the province investments, management, experience and employment already established, and to prevent the economic waste involved in establishing new forest industries."

The politicians had orchestrated a scheme to create new industry in a manner that impaired the stable growth of existing industry. This initial allocation was to unleash the greatest assembly of quick-buck artists ever given free rein in British Columbia. What the politicians did was provide, for nothing, a franchise to particular manipulators that gave them an enormous capital gain. The extent of the gift to New York-based Celanase Corporation, in current dollars, is astounding. The annual cut on this licence, along with another promised at the same time and awarded later, came to about 3.2 million cubic metres. For the sake of comparison, consider the compensation offered by the government to Western Forest Products after a portion of its Tree Farm Licence was taken away on Moresby Island. Western was offered $98 per cubic metre, but claimed a value of $317. Using these numbers, in 1947 the Liberals in the coalition government presented Celanese with a gift worth between $313 million and $1 billion — before the laws permitting it were even passed.

It was this kind of giveaway that attracted hustlers and con artists from far and wide, experts at manipulating the ethics of politicians and public servants alike.

Years later, Orchard acknowledged his oversight in a limited way:

> I did not foresee capital gains possibilities but from
> an economic point of view I couldn't get disturbed when

it promptly did develop. The security of tenure, and other features, were enormously valuable but I had never been able to evolve any alternative scheme under which the public treasury could have collected directly the sums involved. If the treasury didn't profit directly it would profit in the long run, and certainly it didn't lose anything. This feature was, however, one of the factors most favoured by the critics.

There are still apologists for the Tree Farm Licence system in this province who will argue that this kind of giveaway was justified for its value in establishing new industry in the province — that some giveaways were necessary to attract investment capital Celanese and other large companies could bring to BC. In this context it is instructive to follow the evolution of TFL 1.

As part of the deal, Celanese built a pulp mill near Prince Rupert. It was to use what were called pulp logs, but turned out to be sawlogs. Celanese later built a similar pulp mill at Castlegar, in the interior wet belt, to consume "defective" logs: these were actually sawlogs as well, from another TFL.

These two franchises to public property gave Celanese a windfall opportunity to raise capital and invest it elsewhere in the world. The operation evolved into a worldwide conglomerate financed by BC-generated capital, while the BC operations were bled white. In BC, Celanese shouldered citizen business aside and victimized neighbours who operated nearby sawmills and plywood plants, forcing several out of existence when their access to timber disappeared. Celanese operated with outdated technology and absentee management, and denied local management the right to function competently. Within twenty years, Celanese had run a magnificent forest treasure into the ground and put it up for sale.

Between January 1948 and August 1951 I had an office in the Department of Finance, only a few steps from the legislature, so on many occasions I went to listen to the MLAs debate forestry issues. Unfortunately, these were the days before *Hansard*; the speeches are not recorded. Some MLAs were perceptive and genuinely concerned. Backbenchers and even a few cabinet ministers knew that the TFL plan was the wrong course, and that it would encourage a monopoly that would destroy public equity, if not the forest, while destroying opportunities for citizen business. Some hardy MLAs warned from both sides of the speaker's podium that politicians and politics would end up financed by industrial fixers, in exchange for the allocation and control of public timber.

A few weeks before I arrived in Victoria, the leadership of the coalition had disintegrated and Byron "Boss" Johnson, a respected businessman and MLA, became Liberal premier. Johnson was persuaded to use Orchard's sustained yield program as a means of checking the rising popularity of the socialists. Within a few months his government had issued TFL 2. The public lands involved were the islands in Johnstone Strait, a new forest which had grown in after late nineteenth-century logging. On these islands stood some of the most valuable naturally produced new forest in the province and, at the time the TFL was granted, pockets of mature timber bypassed during logging.

This was the area the Celanese delegation had been after in 1947, but they had been turned down. The area was included in a public working circle under the management of the Forest Service, and the mature timber was reserved for the large, well-established independent logging industry. Filberg had been unsuccessful in persuading his Liberal government friends to grant the area to Celanese, but now he was trying again. He appeared with a delegation from another US corporation that had no established operations in the province—Crown Zellerbach.

Orchard was strongly opposed to designating this area as a TFL, and he knew there would be howls of outrage from small local businesses already working there. But behind Orchard's back, and in spite of his warnings that it was being done in an illegal manner, Hart proceeded with the Crown Zellerbach proposal and Johnson awarded it.

Bowing to the inevitable, Orchard consoled himself that TFL met his central objective of gaining control of private land: Filberg had combined 193,000 acres of land owned by his company, Canadian Western Lumber, with 297,000 acres of public land containing a forty-year-old second growth crop.

But John Hart and his forest minister, E.T. Kenney, committed a further violation of statutory intent. They declared the mature crop on the private lands exempt from harvesting restrictions until 1984. This allowed Crown Zellerbach to side-step sustained yield in the mature zone for a period of thirty-five years. In this way, Filberg obtained 297,000 acres of public property — young forest — at no cost, and without having to practise sustained yield forestry for thirty-five years after the allocation. Sloan's recommendations were violated. Orchard's capitulation to political "buy and sell" released the TFL on a shady and sometimes sordid path. There was a clear signal that political deals could be made, regardless of the law. Orchard did nothing except to complain in the privacy of his memoirs.

Orchard continued to regard loggers as a major impediment to sustained yield forestry. This belief appears repeatedly in his memoirs: "forest management had come to British Columbia and the small logger found himself on the way out. He squealed like a stuck pig and blamed everything and everybody other than the real cause. He gave the Forest Service and government some anxious times and did his best to kill forest management." Orchard went so far as to say, "The chief sources of failure of the system I think, were the failure of the smaller operators to take advantage of the chance to establish themselves. They dissipated chances and energies in destructive, futile criticism and opposition. They wanted utterly impossible pie."

The truth is that the independent logger had his throat cut

by Orchard's policy as it evolved. Orchard's distaste for the logger is an integral part of the Tree Farm Licence, which eliminated a competitive log market and failed to provide for cost-effective, professional silviculture. The scheme broadsided the logger who, like a wheat farmer, harvests a mature crop, clears the debris and prepares the soil for the replacement crop. In this work the logger cannot waste any of the mature crop. He must sort his logs by species and grades appropriate to end-uses to maximize sales income and improve his bottom line. He must sell in a market where the price paid for each log category is maximized by the competitive force of open-auction bidding. Orchard's concept aborted all of this.

Accordingly, the resident business logger — the primary silvicultural tool of the forester — was committed to the ash can by official policy, and BC's standards of silviculture rank among the lowest in the world. The established logging industry was denied Tree Farm Licences, except in a few cases which were politically ordered "to show that the little man could participate" — such as TFLs 3 and 5. But it was too late. The allocation of Tree Farm Licences 1 and 2 had mapped the road.

By the time Orchard dictated his post-retirement memoirs, it was clear that the Tree Farm Licence, as he had conceived it, was in trouble. It had been misused to allocate enormous areas to operations that were never considered in the plans. The province's most prestigious forester and industrialist, H.R. MacMillan, had denounced it for further use on the south coast. The new minister, Ray Williston, tossed out the former chief forester's organizational structure in the Forest Service, and refused to use Tree Farm Licences as an instrument to develop the interior pulp industry. In his memoirs, Orchard attacks and blames a variety of people — Fisher, the new Social Credit government, the independent loggers — but never once does he criticize the Liberal coalition politicians who sold his dream down the river before it was even written into the statutes.

The lessons from those years have not been learned. Much later, as chief executive officer of the Canadian manufacturing operations of Triangle Pacific Corporation, a major US lumber trading company, I examined Celanese at the request of my directors and reported it to be a skeleton needing wholesale realignment. I recommended my employer shun such a basket case. Unlimited cheap timber, obsolete technology, uneconomic man-day productivity due to wasteful technology and disheartened local management — these were only the visible defects.

In the early 1970s, under the leadership of David Barrett, BC's first socialist government exercised good judgment in purchasing Celanese. The government was responding to a need for local control and a business plan that incorporated skilled management and the real world of commerce. With the authority and muscle of government, that company could have been turned around. New life could have been breathed into local sawmills, plywood manufacturing, transport and logging companies — the entire business community that had been left damaged by the behaviour of Celanese.

Then the Social Credit Party, led by Bill Bennett, was elected in BC in 1975. This crew created British Columbia Resources Investment Corporation (BCRIC) and announced that private ownership would correct the folly of socialism. The Celanese operation was folded into BCRIC, with a board of directors selected for their commitment to the star of Social Credit. The new company promptly went into coal mining and oil drilling speculation in faraway places, including the North Sea. BCRIC failed. The company lost a bundle of its own and its investors' money.

Eventually, the Nishga Native Tribal Council, concerned about the neglect of the TFL lands in the Nass Valley, undertook an investigation that revealed a serious violation of silvicultural obligations.

In 1986 Bill Vander Zalm assumed leadership of the Social

Credit Party and became premier. His first forest minister, Jack Kempf, was removed from office, allegedly for expense account irregularities, after announcing his intention to sell at least half the public timber at public auction. Vander Zalm then appointed professional forester David Parker to succeed Kempf. When Parker became one of the local managers of the transformed Celanese company, by this time renamed Westar, he tried to implement a plan that would greatly increase the number of Tree Farm Licences. This was quickly halted by widespread public opposition. The first Tree Farm Licence was only an omen of what was to come.

I enjoyed my three and one half years with Fisher and his forest land tax initiative. It is gratifying to me that the concept was applied in other forest jurisdictions in North America, and that Fisher's problem in capital funding was resolved. But once that was achieved, I found that an office in the finance wing of the legislative building was dull stuff. I like to be in the forest, not in an office. In early 1951 the H.R. MacMillan company, which owned forest land, asked me to plan a forest management schedule for them. It was a challenge that few foresters had tackled in British Columbia. It was beyond the dreams of most Canadian foresters in 1951, and it remains so today.

CHAPTER 10

W.A.C. Bennett and Company Arrive on the Scene

When I reported for work at the H.R. MacMillan Export Company Limited on the Monday after Labour Day, 1951, my first task was to open an office at the Harmac pulp mill near Nanaimo. I arrived there just in time to receive a report of a fire on Mount Benson, west of Nanaimo. The fire had been started by careless hunters who had entered the area from south of Parksville. Overnight the fire had spread along both sides of the mountain. Canadian Western Lumber Company sent in fire-fighters from the west side and MacMillan crews attacked the east face of the mountain on the Nanaimo side. By morning it was extremely dangerous to have men in front of the tornado-like advance, and many MacMillan people had to retreat east and south to a road at the base of the mountain.

I was assigned by the fire boss to deliver two bulldozers to the high ground on the east flank, where several men using hand tools worked to expose raw soil as a fire guard. I was unknown in the company and a complete stranger to the crew.

123

On arrival I saw men scratching a pathetic, narrow path through thick, breast-high second growth Douglas fir. That pitchy, thick foliage explodes when it burns, creating a thirty-mile-an-hour suction of air that gives the fire even more momentum. I had fought such fires with my father in the Fraser Valley many times.

The men were in danger and no one on site was in charge. I told them to retreat to the road and help unload the two tractors, then I radioed the fire boss to describe the situation. He authorized me to lead the two bulldozers side by side straight down the mountain to clear a wide path through the firs. The exercise took nearly six hours, by which time the leading edge of the fire, about half a mile wide, was extended in a long point to a spot near the bottom of the south slope of Mount Benson. I knew from experience that when the leading edge of a running fire narrows to a point, air is drawn in from both flanks to support the point. In that circumstance, a back fire along the flank starves the point of the fire, and a fire guard like a wide road is critical for setting a back fire.

The fire boss was H.S. Berryman, a MacMillan vice-president who had started employment as a timekeeper in a logging camp. At the outbreak of the fire he had come to Nanaimo and set up a headquarters. I had not met him, and I had just started my first day on the MacMillan payroll. My radio call did not raise a response.

In a military situation, when you are at the front and action is required, you act according to your best judgment or there may not be a tomorrow. Without wasting any more time on the radio, I lit the back fires along the fire side of the wide swath I had cut in the dense trees. In moments the back fires were drawn away from my fire guard by the air being sucked into the leading edge of the main fire. I knew it was going to work.

Then the radio roared out with the voice of the Canadian Western fire boss from Nanaimo Lake Camp, who demanded to know "Who in the hell is lighting back fires?"

Before I could answer, the calm, disciplined Harry Berryman responded. "Don't get excited. You do your side, we do this one."

"What kind of fool would light more fire?" the western flank man roared back.

Berryman calmly replied, "We are in charge on the east side. When you put your west side out come and talk about it."

By nightfall the fire was stopped at the Nanaimo Lakes road.

Days later I met Berryman for the first time. He said, "So you are the guy who lit the back fire. I had to make it sound like an approved and official initiative or the Canadian Western people would have been after us like tigers. I am glad your plan worked out or at least appeared to work out."

A few days later at a post-fire conference, we reviewed our actions and assessed the damage to company property. Berryman called each participant into his office, thanked him for the hard, risky work, and handed out a thank-you note in the form of a bonus cheque. I had been an employee of the H.R. MacMillan Export Company for five days and I had yet to obtain my first salary cheque, but that day I received a bonus of four hundred dollars.

I never dreamed that a senior vice-president of a big company would get out of his office, take charge of a fire and stick up for an employee he had never met. It would have been easy for Berryman to disown me and let me take the rap if the back fire had not worked. But that was not his style. His people were hired to take the initiative and to deal with the situation at hand. Doing the right thing rather than the wrong thing was appreciated, but in those days do-nothings did not last long as employees of the MacMillan company.

A few weeks later I learned that the MacMillan company had bought that land and timber just days before the fire started, but that the cheque had not been delivered. By the time the cheque arrived, MacMillan had paid for devastated land. My crews replanted the site and it is with pride that I drive by it today, a thirty-eight-year-old forest ready for selective thinning of saleable timber.

Just before the election that installed W.A.C. Bennett, when I was an employee of MacMillan and a resident of Nanaimo, I felt duty-bound to participate in politics at the constituency level. One Saturday, which was then a work day, I had taken time off to hand-dig a sewer line for the house I was building. In the course of the day I was visited first by the Liberal candidate, then the Conservative. Both sought support in the forthcoming provincial election. The Liberal was an old man and a supporter of the defeated coalition. The Conservative was a medical doctor with no previous political experience. He was young, genial and willing to condemn the defeated coalition. He was also prepared to accept a socialist government if that was the alternative to a failure of the Conservatives to win the election.

The young doctor, Larry Giovando, took off his jacket, borrowed gumboots from me and stayed the afternoon to help finish the sewer connection. In return I agreed to work on his campaign and write a series of community-oriented speeches for him. My wife objected to my burning the midnight oil, one-fingering a typewriter to produce speeches. For a while, though, the doctor convinced her of the merits of the project.

Giovando was a man with great charm and little political sophistication. He was as likely to appear at a Baptist Church Temperance meeting discussing the wealth his family had acquired rum-running on Saltspring Island, as he was to attend a meeting of ex-soldiers at a Canadian Legion picnic and preach the evils to be found in a glass of beer. However, he was elected, and to my wife's horror I agreed to write a speech for the doctor's first address to the legislature. In it he expressed his opposition to current forest policy. It was not long before the naïve doctor became an expert on forestry in the legislature.

Then the spokesman for the Liberals wanted to engage the doctor's ghost-writer to help them attack the new Social Credit government. My services were offered, and suddenly I was working a triple shift. Just when my wife was about to go home to her mother, along came H.R. MacMillan to save the day.

From time to time, it was MacMillan's habit to engage a room in the Empress Hotel and invite MLAs to lunch. He liked one of the doctor's speeches on forest policy so much that the doctor was invited. MacMillan congratulated him for his fine, thoughtful series of speeches, and encouraged the doctor to make another speech to underline a point regarding the substance of a Tree Farm Licence contract. MacMillan explained that a licence should not be allocated unless the recipient included all his private lands. He then said that TFL 2 had been awarded improperly because private lands had not been committed; it was improper that public lands had been allocated. The good doctor, not sure of the significance of the point, responded "I'll ask Ian Mahood what he thinks of that, and if he agrees I'll do what you ask."

H.R. made a strange grunting sound and discreetly went on to discuss another topic. Then, with obvious agitation, he abruptly excused the doctor MLA. Minutes later, at the North West Bay Logging Division near Parksville, I got instructions to telephone a Victoria number immediately. *"Mahood!"* The voice at the other end sounded like a volcano erupting. I had been warned about such explosions on H.R.'s part, and I knew there would be trouble if I did not have a rational explanation. I outlined the circumstances. The voice, more subdued, said in as terse a manner as I had heard from H.R., "Get out of this deal in Victoria. You will get the company into politics. Get out of town until the budget debate is finished." That was end of the conversation.

I reported to my boss in Vancouver, and that evening I boarded the last ferry to the mainland and drove all night to Portland, Oregon to a logging convention. Months later, H.R. discussed his fear that bribery had been involved in the allocation of Tree Farm Licences 1 and 2. He stipulated that no one employed by the MacMillan Company was to be involved in politics. I told my doctor friend that my political activities had to end.

As a parting piece of advice, I suggested that in the 1953 provincial election, in which W.A.C. Bennett sought a workable majority, the doctor should claim overwork and book off sick. I reasoned that people voting second and third preference would give those votes to Larry because he was young and popular, and they would feel somewhat accountable for the exhaustion imposed on him in the legislative session. For a good part of the campaign he rested in Palm Springs, California, "debilitated from overwork." As sure as the sun rises and sets, in the preferential voting system second and third choices cross party lines and elect the candidate with the greatest appeal to men or finest rapport with women. Larry's political views contributed little, but he was assured of election by the admirers who gave him second ballot votes. Such is the mystery and hazard of the form of ballot that first elected a government headed by W.A.C. Bennett. Significantly, Bennett abandoned the innovation after he won a majority in his second campaign as Social Credit leader.

It is useful to recall that Bennett headed a strange list of MLAs, some of whom behaved as though they had put their shoes on for the first time when they entered the legislature. And, in fairness to W.A.C., it must be said that he inherited the Tree Farm Licence system. It was not prudent to terminate the program and cancel the licences either issued or committed before he came to office; such an action would have shattered investor confidence in BC. Money from stock market sources would have dried up, and institutional lenders who provided money for roads, railroads and hydro development would also have become nervous.

Such expansion of the provincial economy was a plan already taking shape in the mind of Premier Bennett. He could not dismantle the Tree Farm Licence program without a visible cause that would be understood and accepted by institutional money lenders, as well as by the voters. A politician like Bennett knew the idea of sustained yield forestry appealed to voters — it gave them the impression their equity in the forest was being protected.

Bennett had to mould a group of inexperienced members of the legislature into a government that could consolidate its electoral support. Harmony, not confrontation on forest policy, was the logical and prudent course. It is likely that Bennett knew the coalition's election campaign had been generously financed by recipients and hopeful recipients of Tree Farm Licences, and the knowledge would not have been distasteful to him. In any event, besides the cases of TFLs 1 and 2, which can be classified as horrors, there were others less appalling, and even a few that had merit. At this early stage in their development, there was no obvious reason to condemn those TFLs approved by the defeated government. Chief Forester and Deputy Minister C.D. Orchard was a saintly figure in the public mind; a politician as perceptive as Bennett would not have interfered with him. Besides, Bennett understood that the central thrust of forest policy was the regaining of public control over forests. Private companies would then have a contractual commitment to log without waste, reforest the lands they denuded and control forest fires. That was the public perception of forest policy that had been articulated by Chief Justice Gordon Sloan. Bennett had no reason to foresee that the Tree Farm Licence, like the wooden horse that conquered Troy, would eventually demand that British Columbians feed it with taxpayers' dollars, while it nibbled the forest lands of BC into economic impotence.

Bennett had a problem, though. C.D. Orchard had a built-in dislike — hatred might be a more accurate term — of Bennett's regime. Orchard's memoirs, written after his retirement, are explicit and uncompromising.

I would not have credited the character of our new cabinet. We had been accustomed to deal with men of character and ideals. . . . We drew as our minister, the infamous, treacherous, R.E. Sommers. . . . His forestry training had consisted in seasonal work for a few summers with the Forest Service. In my opinion the Social Credit government was a one man administration. Ministers were nonentities who referred the simplest routine matters to Mr. Bennett, the premier, and parroted his decisions.

I was told and apparently the government credited it that I had actively sought the Liberal nomination in Victoria.

I was told civil servants had no conception of economics. We were to do purely routine work. The government would instruct us in all else. . . .

In January, 1953, the minister instructed me to give him a selection of two licences [TFL] one small one to be approved and a big one to be disallowed.

Orchard apparently found this kind of political maneuvering on the part of the Social Credit government distasteful, despite his own previous involvement in similar projects for the coalition government. Most notably, two very small licences, TFLs 3 and 5, had been issued "to show that we do not exclude small operators from the forest policy." Both applicants for these licences had been solicited by Orchard.

"The government [Social Credit] supported the principle of forest management," Orchard continued, "but, from complete lack of individual or corporate character, they floundered between politics, principle and cupidity. Shortly they began sell [Tree Farm Licences] for what they could get in under cover graft."

For example, there was the Robert Sommers bribery case. The forests around Tofino, on the west coast of Vancouver

Island, had been designated as a Public Working Circle in which timber would be harvested by market loggers under competitively obtained timber sales. The lands would be managed by the Forest Service. Under Sommers, the first Socred forest minister, the area was granted to BC Forest Products as TFL 22. It was later proved in court that Sommers accepted a bribe.

Quite apart from the legal and ethical considerations, there were proper forest management reasons why the licence should not have been issued. There were defects in the management and working plan that violated professional forestry practice. At the time, Section 33, Subsection 5 of the Forest Act stated: "The management and working plan prepared under provisions of subsection (4) shall be submitted for the approval of the chief forester, and no management licence shall be issued until the management and working plan has been approved." Orchard never did approve the plan. Since 1912, when the Forest Act became operational, it had been widely understood that political considerations would never overrule forest management decisions of the professional chief forester. As chief forester, Orchard had an obligation not only to refuse to approve Tree Farm Licence 22, but to take the next step — to block its approval.

It should be noted that the statement Orchard credits to Bennett concerning his Liberal party connections was not without foundation. Orchard was a well-known Victoria Liberal and, while he may not have sought the nomination actively, it was offered to him by John Hart and he apparently accepted. He was not the dispassionate civil servant he liked to present himself as, but a senior bureaucrat with a political agenda and links to a party that was fighting to regain power.

The Sommers affair touched me indirectly when I was busy at MacMillan Bloedel, developing forest management plans for private lands to be integrated into Tree Farm Licences. At that stage, despite H.R. MacMillan's deep dislike of the TFL, it was recommended that we apply for public timber lands adjacent to and intermingled with our private corporate properties. This would prevent other parties from making an application. We applied for particular corners of public land intermingled with M & B lands on the west coast of Vancouver Island.

While no contract had been signed, a memorandum of understanding had been worked out with Orchard's office. One day, without warning, a junior official of the Forest Service hand-delivered a message that BC Forest Products Limited had been issued a Tree Farm Licence that included timber within the area approved for M & B. We were stunned. BCFP was an independent company and had no financial relations with M & B. However, M & B had a contract to sell BCFP's products and senior executives of BCFP were former employees of M & B. We were also surprised that Orchard had unilaterally repudiated his approval of areas assigned to M & B.

Sommers was eventually found guilty of taking a bribe, but other unsavoury actions far more significant went unpunished. Some day the other aspects of the Sommers case may surface.

In late February 1955 Gordon Gibson, the Liberal MLA and former west coast logger, threw down the gauntlet with a speech in the legislature charging "money talks" — a suggestion that more government members than Sommers were on the take. Within two weeks the cabinet benches were in disarray. Ministers were backing, filling and stubbing each others' toes. It was a government in deep trouble.

Bennett appointed Judge Arthur Lord to investigate Gibson's allegations. Wilson Gray, who subsequently went to jail for serving as the conduit to the bribery, was not called to testify, nor was Sommers. Gordon Gibson's lawyer attended the hearings, saying the "money talks" allegation was not intended to refer to any individual or his honesty but simply to underline that Tree Farm Licence policy favoured big companies and discriminated against small ones. Orchard, with the mantle of respectability conferred by his position as deputy minister and chief forester, attended. He said he knew nothing about dishonesty in the granting of Tree Farm Licences.

On March 9, 1955, Judge Lord reported no impropriety on anyone's part in the issuing of Tree Farm Licences, and said that in making his comments, Gordon Gibson was not being specific, but was only generalizing: companies and men with plenty of money had an advantage over those with little money.

Gibson had the documentary evidence of bribery, but was not yet ready to release it when the inquiry was called. Caught off guard and hoping to buy time, Gibson resigned his seat, forcing a by-election. He declared he would test public opinion "on the issue of this money-mad Social Credit government, tumbling all over itself to make grants of our crown resources in perpetuity for the short term gain of immediate investment, against a policy insisting on a plan for participation by the small operator, and the retention of our resource for future genera-tions." On September 12, Gibson lost the by-election. He had been out-manoeuvered by Bennett: he had been forced to conduct the debate in a partisan political arena, which prevented the public from taking it too seriously.

The premier then appointed Chief Justice Sloan to conduct another royal commission on forestry. Sloan rejected evidence submitted by Gibson's lawyer, David Sturdy, and lawyers acting for Sommers sued Sturdy for slander. That kept the matter out of the press and public mind, because nothing could be said while the slander suit was before the courts. Bennett knew the truth: Sommers was a "dead duck." Bennett's damage control plan needed just one more leg to stand on, a new, fresh face for minister of forests.

On February 17, 1956, Sommers rose from his accustomed seat in the legislature, beside Bennett, and started a speech which the premier had ordered must end with his resignation as minister of lands and forests. The unhappy, unfortunate man told his listeners the courts were the proper place to prove one's innocence, and he was going to protect his honour through civil action against his detractors, whose motives were based on nothing but political malice. He declared his unwillingness to put his fate in the hands of a royal commission on forestry, because such a forum could be used to publish heresy and half-truths, against which he would have no defence. He turned to Premier Bennett's empty chair and resigned as minister.

Soon after Sommers had begun speaking, Bennett had passed a note to Education Minister Ray Williston, asking him to go to the premier's office. Bennett joined him a few minutes later, put on his black homburg and ushered him to a waiting car, whose chauffeur drove the two men to Government House. There Williston was sworn in as minister of lands and forests. The next day, Williston was seated at Bennett's right and began a distinguished, productive and remarkable career.

Some weeks later my office telephone rang and Williston introduced himself, then requested a meeting in a convenient forest area. I fumbled and must have sounded disinterested, but I was mindful of MacMillan's restriction on contacts between his employees and politicians. I telephoned my boss in Vancouver for approval. Williston met me in Nanaimo and we spent several days of relaxed travel and discussion, using M & B's guest house at Alberni as a headquarters. We visited the forest area of the Ash River, where I had done the first reforestation in Canada using a helicopter to spread seed and apply fertilizer. We discussed silviculture, organization in the Forest Service and lines of accountability. Out of our conversation a personal friendship developed that has endured many years, in spite of my sometimes critical comments about the public policy that he expedited.

Williston's ethical foundations were honourable. While in office, his proposals spanned forestry, lands, water resources, hydro development, parks and recreation, the environment and, in particular, the burden of developing a viable interior forest industry capable of competing in the rich United States market. In doing this, he managed to avoid using the Tree Farm

Licence concept, which he disliked and distrusted as a vehicle for economic development, particularly in the interior of BC.

Meanwhile, Orchard, the architect of the system that so quickly became a vehicle for bribery, corruption and assets grabs by major corporations, had ridden out the storm. He retired quietly in 1956. For several months of the following year, he worked at UBC on a forest history project, which unfortunately he attempted to use as an instrument for vindicating the forest policies he had brought into existence.

Orchard had only a few years remaining to serve when the Sommers case hit the headlines. The proper thing for him to do was to put his job on the line for the sake of the principle when TFL 22 was awarded, even if he had had another century until retirement. If he had evidence the government was "selling Tree Farm Licences for what they could get in under cover graft," he had a public duty as a civil servant to make the evidence available. During the Lord investigation, he had another opportunity — and responsibility — to set the record straight, but he failed to do so. Making the allegation in his memoirs was not enough.

I believe that Orchard sidestepped the obligation of a professional forester implied in the Magna Carta concept of forestry, if not the intent of the statute governing the role of the chief forester. It was clear from the beginning that Tree Farm Licences provoked political favouritism.

For more than thirty years, the province has laboured under an unfair and iniquitous forest tenure system that is at the root of our current conflicts over forest land management. The skeletons that Chief Forester Orchard helped stuff into the closet in the early 1950s are coming out to haunt us today.

CHAPTER 11

Launching a Silvicultural Program on Private Lands

The H.R. MacMillan Export Company Limited was founded in 1919 as a marketing agent for British Columbia lumber, railway ties, plywood and similar commodities, which were sold to worldwide customers. It was so successful that a subsidiary shipping company was established to transport the products of BC mills to foreign customers.

At the same time the MacMillan Company started, the major coastal sawmills formed a marketing alliance against MacMillan. This alliance sought to take over the sales of BC forest products from the American brokers who had always dominated the business. Eventually a fierce competition developed between MacMillan and his opponents, which attempted to cut off his lumber supply. He responded by acquiring timber and a manufacturing capacity.

To every challenge there was a dramatic response by MacMillan and his partner, W.J. Van Dusen. Through the Depression of the 1930s, when the US placed tariff barriers on Canadian lumber, British Columbia producers had great difficulty; some

136

of them vanished forever. While it was a struggle, MacMillan's effort matched his determination. He battled on, winning the sale of railway ties to India, or a major lumber order in South Africa. Its growth was limited, but MacMillan's company did not lose momentum. Through the selective acquisition of manufacturing capacity and timber, MacMillan maintained shipments to hard-won customers. Driven by his unflagging energy and the skill of Van Dusen, the enterprise prospered. MacMillan's opponents began to stumble.

When World War II erupted, MacMillan men contributed their abilities to overseas military duties. Those not in service worked double-shift duty supplying lumber, timbers and plywood for military needs. MacMillan, not of military age, "enlisted" to serve first as timber controller and then as chairman of the Wartime Shipping Board. In late 1944, with the war's end in sight and shipping well organized, he began visiting Vancouver regularly to relieve his hard-pressed partner and staff, and to resume the battle with his competitors.

Shareholders in the MacMillan company received a surprise in the annual report for 1944. It contained a bland but electrifying statement: "H.R. MacMillan Export Company was appointed managing agent for the Victoria Lumber and Manufacturing Company whose large timber holdings of high quality and excellent factories will be a source of strength to all our enterprises."

MacMillan had acquired control of the largest and most wealthy component of his competitors' alliance. This dealt his competitors a punitive, and in due course, mortal blow.

A second announcement in 1944, viewed with interest and alarm by senior officials in the provincial Forest Service, reported steps taken in the company to establish a corporate forestry division, aimed at applying silviculture to privately owned land. J.D. Gilmore, a distinguished first-generation forester from Ontario, was hired to head up the program. The slow-paced forestry monopoly enjoyed by government was about to meet a serious challenge.

In 1951, just a decade after starting private forestry at Franklin River near Port Alberni, Prentice Bloedel negotiated a merger with MacMillan's company. This merger was neither a conquest nor a capitulation by either party. It was a sound plan to form a major Canadian forest company capable of raising the capital needed to install modern forest technology. This technology was required to maximize the value of forest products, allowing penetration of markets other than those interested in raw lumber. Investment in silviculture was a key item on the agenda. Before the merger, both companies had launched reforestation programs in their respective operating areas. MacMillan acted first in 1936 by instituting patch logging to induce natural seeding, and Bloedel had started plantations in the early 1940s.

With the merger, I became manager of Forestry Operations, accountable for silviculture. One of my first experiences in this capacity was to serve as tour guide in some of the second-crop forests. C.D. Orchard, the chief forester, had been invited to join Mr. MacMillan and Mr. Bloedel on a tour of the new company's lands. The company sought assurance from Orchard that public land, intermingled with the private land of the merged companies, would not be allocated in Tree Farm Licences to other parties. The company also wanted to tell Orchard that, while it did not agree with the Tree Farm Licence concept, as soon as the technical and field work could be finished, a defensive application to protect our position would be filed.

Orchard was genial and comfortable as H.R. drove his Rolls Royce along the old railway grades which had been converted to logging roads. The roads were narrow and of low quality, with fore and aft planks on cross-ties at the culverts and bridges. One had to approach them full square to be sure of smooth passage — in fact, to be sure of any passage at all.

Designated as navigator, I sat in the front seat. My only contribution was to hold my breath as H.R. approached a corner or lined up to charge a bridge. I could tell by the rise and fall of breathing in the back seat that Orchard and Bloedel were contributing in like fashion. H.R., a skilled driver in his own unusual way, never so much as dragged the bottom of his car on a rock or log chunk, many of which protruded from the old railway grades. Somewhere near Coleman Creek, where I had worked as a logger in 1936 and which had once been the scene of devastation by fire, glossy green Douglas fir seedlings grew above the stumps that were former forest giants.

H.R. stopped the Rolls and delivered a speech on the effectiveness of natural regeneration through patch logging. He was a master of rich and eloquent language. However, I knew this was a plantation established by Bloedel in 1941, and the silence in the back seat from Prentice Bloedel was notable. Orchard purred with satisfaction.

As quietly as I could, and without wanting to appear the smart young man before such wisdom, I said, "I think there has been some plantation along the old railway grade. What do you think, H.R.?" The answer was a commentary on the difference between natural and plantation seedlings in terms that placed some doubt on my competence as a forester. The silence in the back seat was broken by Bloedel, who said, "H.R., it is one of our plantations." I pointed out that there would be a sign on a post just along the grade which would settle the debate with authority. H.R., in silence, drove just a bit more erratically around the next corner and crossed a rickety bridge over a clear, cool creek. The sign was there for all to read: "Plantation, 1941." We all vacated the Rolls to sip from the creek.

Orchard, strictly a bystander, had made no comment. Reforestation was not on his mind. At every opportunity he expressed expansive views on the advantages of Tree Farm Licences. He was selling and he knew he had reluctant buyers.

Bloedel then requested we travel to the Ash River to examine

reforestation resulting from patch logging and naturally in-
duced regeneration. H.R. got into the back seat, Bloedel came
forward and I was assigned the driver's role.

For the first time in my life I was driving a Rolls Royce
product. To have that luxury on a rough, abandoned railway
grade where one could drag the bottom out of the car without
even trying, seemed to me a hazardous introduction. My
tenure with the newly formed MacMillan Bloedel could have
been extraordinarily short had I crumpled a fender. Happily,
we made it to the Ash River area and a logged patch surrounded
by mature timber. Young trees, lush, bright and healthy, covered the site. I waited beside the Rolls while MacMillan plunged
into the young stand, followed by the august chief forester of
BC and, with equal enthusiasm, Prentice Bloedel.

I waited, reflecting on my good fortune to have spent a day
with three interesting men. Suddenly a snap of pain struck at
man's most important and vital appendage. A quick inspection
revealed a wood tick buried in the end of it. As a non-smoker
I was defenceless, needing a cigarette to drive out the insect.
Only Orchard smoked, and then only occasionally. On his
return to the car I took him aside to explain my predicament.
He gave me a cigarette and I retreated behind the Rolls, while
the others waited. The glowing cigarette murdered the wood
tick, the most hazardous beast in the daily work of a dirt
forester. There are foresters who have never had rain in their
lunch buckets and many who have never had a wood tick in a
critical extremity. MacMillan, back behind the wheel of the
Rolls, held forth authoritatively on flora and fauna, including
an eloquent discussion of wood tick attacks on foresters.

I have a scar that remains to this day, an odd memento of
possibly the only time those three men met and enjoyed themselves while discussing forestry. And the Rolls survived. I
encountered it on other occasions when H.R. preempted my
weekends with my family to examine my stewardship in his
forest land.

After the merger of the two companies in 1951, the Forestry Operations Division became a key corporate tool. Its duties ranged from determining the best use of mature timber, to planning reforestation, to controlling silvicultural procedures such as location and timing of logging, slash burning, selection of seed trees and other steps to assure regeneration. The members of the committee were the senior directors: Hoffmeister, MacMillan, Van Dusen, Bloedel and, initially, Sidney Smith. Staff members were Angus MacBean, in charge of forest policy and relations with the Forest Service, and Keith Shaw, manager of (Land) Properties. I was the manager of Forestry Operations.

It was my job to prepare agenda items, position papers and recommendations for action. Each committee member received a copy one week before a meeting, which was ordinarily held once a month. All were expected to study the material and go to the meeting with an opinion, if not a conclusion. It was bad form to arrive late or be unprepared to discuss and vote on a recommendation. Debate was thorough and sometimes arduous, and it was always followed by a prompt decision. The authority to carry out a proposal had a stimulating effect on our confidence. If the results were poorer than expected, even if a disaster resulted, the committee made no complaint, provided the member had followed the approved course of action: we were all in it together. If there was a deviation from the agreed-upon course, ineffective follow-up, or failure to report a problem, only the Almighty on high could redeem the man.

By 1952 the company, in defence of its position and cutting rights in public timber, had to make a decision on applications for Tree Farm Licences. We could not endlessly object to the policy while leaving critical forest areas available to competitors. We were forced to submit the appropriate applications. With these on file and approved for processing by the Forest Service, the company could organize its own forest management program on company lands, while protecting its rear in respect to public property.

In light of this new situation, I drafted a list of priorities. My plans were approved by the Committee with some amendment. These were my ideas:

(1) Fit the product manufacturing and sales program to the species and grades in our forest with a view to minimizing waste in the slash.

M & B mills were to be adjusted to fit the range of species and log sizes within the corporate forest. The log trading division would work to sell surplus log categories taken from company forests and buy from the open log market to cover any shortages. Besides increasing profits this would reduce logging slash, essential to follow-up with crop replacing silviculture.

There were no dissenters on the committee. In the field, however, the logging managers didn't like losing their option of high-grading the forest and claiming credit for their efficiency as loggers. They did not want a forester identifying when and where to log. But they didn't have much choice in the matter. The committee had no problem sending the message out to the logging divisions.

(2) Convert from railway logging to truck logging.

This was needed to get the flexibility to achieve the first priority. In addition, it was deemed appropriate to log high elevation areas in the snow-free season and retreat to low elevation sites for winter logging. That increased the work year of logging employees and increased the productivity of capital invested in logging equipment. Dispersal also provided flexibility so that the company could concentrate on getting raw material best suited to fill the orders of the sales department.

Advance knowledge of product output would identify where the sales program needed to concentrate its effort.

(3) Develop an assured supply of tree seed of proven genetic quality as a source of nursery grown plantation seedlings that would be compatible with the areas scheduled for logging.

It was necessary to have enough lead time so supply of suitable seed was available before committing to clear-cut an area.

(4) Bring company-owned lands into a fully stocked, second crop status to qualify for taxation rate of 1 percent on forest crop land instead of the 6 percent applied to denuded areas classified as wild land.

(5) Hire qualified foresters to staff each logging division so that forestry and logging schedules were effectively coordinated.

Slash burning, which was to be a silvicultural tool, would come under control of the accountable professional forester.

(6) Selectively purchase areas of second crop land, bearing stands twenty years and older, to improve the age-class distribution in the second crop forest.

This policy was to apply to land within a fifty-mile radius of the Harmac mill in Nanaimo to shore up the long-term timber supply for that mill.

As I progressed through my list at the committee meeting, H.R. commented on it with enthusiasm, which was more than I had expected. I was a junior in years and an employee of only a few months. I was a second-generation forester sitting in a meeting with two distinguished first-generation professionals, MacMillan and Van Dusen, as well as Prentice Bloedel, who had scientific instincts, and Angus MacBean, a great policy forester. MacBean was in support, but worried about timing and my straight-on approach. He thought I should feel out the committee first. Discussion of the last item led us into an examination of one of the most serious problems of crop replacement forestry. The federal Tax Act did not allow us to write off the cost of reforestation along with other costs of operating the business. Instead, we had to treat it as a capital cost, and our shareholders tended to favour capital investments like mill expansions that produced quicker returns than planting trees. The tax laws meant I could purchase land with a twenty-year-old crop at less than the cost of planting one-year-old seedlings.

All present agreed there must be current expensing of forest replacement. Reforestation cannot be left to the vagaries of nature, Hoffmeister argued. He added, though, that the shareholders would not accept using capital for reforestation if we were to be denied expensing of our forestry costs. He pointed out that we had requested and been denied Orchard's support for a petition to Ottawa.

Then it was suggested I go to Victoria and try to get the support of the Finance Ministry, before going on to Ottawa to lobby the federal government. The next day, MacMillan telephoned C.D. Howe, the minister of industry in Ottawa, to arrange a meeting for me. First I went to Victoria and got assured support from my former employer, Deputy Minister of Finance J.V. Fisher. In Ottawa, after a brief chat with C.D. Howe, I was ushered into the office of a busy deputy minister of taxation.

I started by explaining that sustained yield forestry requires annual expenditure on the land to establish new growth. There was no dispute on that point, but the deputy argued that if he allowed a write-off on forestry costs, he would have to deny a depletion of capital costs on mature timber. We could not expect to write off both the cost to create and the cost to deplete our timber.

I had anticipated such a response, and said, "In the case of privately owned timber we purchased for cash out front, we of course have a capital account. That is being depleted in direct relation to the original cost. There is nothing new in that. It is a legitimate cost of supplying raw material and, thus, fully deductible from gross income earned in the year."

The deputy nodded in apparent agreement.

I continued, "What is new is that we reforest our own land with an annual expenditure for reforestation. When we harvest the new crop you will not be asked to allow us a depletion because we will be on a sustained yield harvesting regime. We make the reforestation expenditure as a cost of staying in business in order to earn money. Therefore, it is proper that we expense that cost in the year we incur the expense."

The deputy thought for a few minutes and replied, "You are entitled to expense the cost of maintaining the business in the year. What you have described can be deemed of that character. We do not need to change the law. I can write an administrative ruling. As you see, I am busy. Would you draft a memo in the language you think appropriate and give me a copy. I will scrutinize it and let it fly."

That night I drafted a proposal. At nine o'clock in the morning, Pacific time, I telephoned Charles Chambers, M & B's taxation expert, to run it by him. He changed some words and I passed the draft to the tax official, who looked it over and thanked me for my help. Within days it was made official. A giant leap had been taken in forest management. It allowed us to practise silviculture on the lands in my charge. I telephoned a report to Hoffmeister. He nearly fell off his chair, an unusual response from that cool and collected old soldier.

In those days, M & B deposited an employee's pay twice a month in a Bank of Commerce account. Shortly after my visit to the tax man, I found I had more money in my paycheque account than I had thought. I went to the paymaster, expecting to straighten out a mistake, but he told me he had instructions to raise my salary, retroactive one month. Hoffmeister admitted he had authorized a raise, and H.R. had suggested the retroactive feature. This was typical of M & B's treatment of its middle-level executives in those days. It was one of the reasons for the success and vigour of the company. Its principals did their homework, and dealt with people one-on-one. If you were not performing, you knew it in a short time. If you were on the ball, you heard about it in the same short time. Unlike many companies, this one had no remote inner circle so far from the ship of state that they didn't know the course on which it was heading.

H.R. MacMillan's enthusiasm for forestry was unbounded. He would poke his nose in periodically, usually on weekends, because in those days he often spent time at his dairy farm near Qualicum. One of my forester scientists, Dr. T.N. Stoate, an Australian the same age as MacMillan, was experimenting with the use of mineral trace elements to stimulate tree growth and increase seed production. H.R. was fascinated and made many weekend excursions to monitor the experiments. He could often be found on his hands and knees measuring minute differences in growth between treated and untreated stock.

After my taxation report to the Forestry and Timber Committee I got approval for all six of the ideas I had outlined. In a few years we bought upwards of 150,000 acres of second crop lands, twenty years or older, at an average cost of $20 per acre, less than the cost of plantation. A forester moved into the administration of each of the logging divisions. Once the land was logged, it came under the care and custody of the company's Forestry Division. We moved into silviculture with many significant firsts on a production scale, rather than an experimental one: helicopter seeding, thinning of immature stands for optimum spacing of trees, helicopter fertilizing with nitrogen pellets, and planting at ten-by-ten-foot spacing. We developed seed orchards and carried out slash burning with a planned silvicultural focus. We did all the essentials for replacing a tree crop. While the Forest Service postulated and other companies were thinking, we were doing.

In purchasing land, I had a crew that did appraisals. I then inspected on my own so I would be informed personally. It was a defensive action, because Hoffmeister, even more than H.R., believed in accountability. There was no way I would recommend purchase without personally examining the property. I had the authority to make a quick purchase up to a particular limit. After that I had to get approval of the Forestry and Timber Committee. As a precaution, I usually got this approval beforehand, if only for the reason that other committee members were always available for informal discussion.

Once I was offered a forty-acre parcel containing a forty-year stand of sawlog size. The cost per acre was double my average, $20, and I had to decide quickly. I telephoned Hoffmeister and told him the particulars. He discussed it with H.R., then telephoned to say that H.R. had some questions for me.

H.R.'s voice came on the line. He was concerned that my average cost per acre was going to double. I was therefore bidding up my own market, which H.R. thought was a bad idea. He said it would end up costing more money in the long run. And anyway, he wanted to know, what made me think it was worth $40 an acre?

I told him the land had usable sawlogs. I said I could log it right then and there and make a profit. H.R. still seemed unconvinced. Finally I said, "H.R., do you mind if I buy it for myself?" "If it's that good," H.R. replied, "you buy it for the company."

I bought the parcel for the company. Then I made a deal with Larry Harris, manager of the Harmac pulp mill. I asked him what price the pulp mills in eastern Canada were paying for eight-foot cord wood. He told me $15 per cord. I said, "I'm going to deliver some cordage."

My crew divided the property into four ten-acre sections. At my direction, one segment was untouched and the other three were thinned, applying different techniques. After paying the harvest and delivery costs I recovered enough money to pay the cost of purchase.

Some months later, H.R. toured with me on one of his weekend look-and-see visits. These informal meetings cut across all normal channels of communication and made it difficult for Hoffmeister who, in military style, always dealt with people through the proper lines of authority. MacMillan had a habit of talking to uninformed people, who would gossip rather than provide him with factual information. On this occasion he wanted to look at the $40-per-acre property. He drove the Rolls Royce up to the centre post of the property, where all of the ten-acre blocks were visible. Before we got out of the car, I explained to H.R. each type of thinning and gave him a sketch of the finances. In some delight, I told him I had recovered the cost of acquisition. He went into orbit, saying I was just trying to show him up as forester: "You are trying to prove I was wrong when I told you not to buy it." Caught off guard, I told him that I had wanted to prove both to myself and to my staff that their economic estimates had been accurate. If they had been wrong I had told my staff I would fire them.

His outburst behind him, MacMillan was somewhat calm again. "Ian," he said, "if you had not done this thinning and proved to your own satisfaction you were right, I would have fired you. If I am wrong it is your job to prove it. We cannot run our forestry program on bright ideas that are ultimately moonbeams. Forestry costs money and we have to be right the first time. There is too much loose paper theory in forest management and not enough work under the tree and on the ground." H.R. did not apologize for his outburst; it was not his style. His employees were expected to be on their toes 110 percent of the time.

After each of these weekend visits to the forestry patch, I would telephone the vice-president whom I reported to and give him a run-down on H.R.'s visit. I would report when and where H.R. had got out his stubby little pencil to make notes in the little book he always carried. I would also ask my boss to inform Hoffmeister. I felt obligated to do this because, according to my military experience, any lapse in correct, formal communication was dangerous. H.R.'s loose style sometimes created misunderstanding and confusion about what the field managers were actually doing. Often the gossip that got through to H.R. was disrupting, a burden for all of the executive people, particularly Hoffmeister.

MacMillan knew he wanted to turn the reins over to younger men. But having done that, he took the reins back at every opportunity. Hoffmeister had in-depth training and experience in corporate organization. He had the unbounded respect of his associates throughout the organization. He was greatly admired, most of all by MacMillan — for years there was almost a father and son relationship between them. The record shows that during Hoffmeister's term as chairman and chief executive officer, the company earned its highest rate of return on capital investment. And this was before the days of subsidy or "sympathetic administration."

One morning, however, H.R. walked in and in one of those peremptory moves that sometimes characterized MacMillan in his later years with the company, told Hoffmeister to clean out his desk by five o'clock. That action unleashed fifteen years of strange and convoluted history, during which the company was severed from its roots in the forest and lurched down an unprofitable, uncertain path. The great loss to BC was the company's leadership in forest management. M & B became just another component of the corporate monopoly — the evil empire that MacMillan himself had been determined to prevent.

In opposing the Tree Farm Licence at the second Sloan Commission, MacMillan described his vision of MacMillan Bloedel's forest management on company-owned lands:

> Individuals and teams from the various production divisions are constantly visiting operations throughout the world to examine new equipment and technology.
>
> A ten-year program to eliminate waste is reaching perfection. Log barkers have been installed, bark and sawdust are used for fuel, all usable sawmill waste is made into chips for company pulp mills. Certain classes of waste, as yet not usable otherwise, go into Pres-to logs and brickettes. Logs unsuitable for sawmills go direct to pulpmills. Completion of the company's pulpmill and paper expansion (currently underway) will see the end of leaving any log in the forest slash, large or small, unless they are half-rotten.
>
> Too little is known about factors influencing the growth of a new crop. Our Forestry Division consists of nine foresters. We need more. They all live in the towns on Vancouver Island. Their time is spent in our logging operations and the areas of new forest we are establishing and protecting. They conduct field examinations year round. They visit and study what foresters have accomplished during the past forty years under similar conditions in neighbouring US states.
>
> We are conducting experiments with trace elements and broadcast spreading of commercial high nitrogen fertilizer to learn if slower growth can be improved at acceptable costs. A tree farm of twenty-five thousand acres is maintained and kept under observation. It is a field laboratory. An amount not over the annual growth is now being logged from it each year.

MacMillan Bloedel Limited's yearly spending on silviculture equals thirty percent of the total expenditure for that purpose by the provincial Forest Service. Obviously the timber owned by the province is so many times greater that the provincial government should supply the money, or get it from the Dominion, for a much greater silvicultural research program.

MacMillan Bloedel Limited brought aerial seeding to British Columbia. A minimum of fifteen hundred acres is planted or seeded yearly.

Forest fire protection is no longer a rule of thumb business. Studies of risk and protective equipment have vastly improved our prospects of preventing and suppressing forest fires before they get away. Fire drills, called without notice, are held frequently on all logging operations. The target is to get water in three minutes on a fire in an active logging operation. Our surprise fire drills are doing it. The company flies a fire patrol daily during fire hazard.

While this statement was being read, I stood at the doorway of the courtroom. I enjoyed the words and reflected that no other company in BC, or in Canada, could honestly describe such a solid forestry program. A private enterprise program far exceeding anything done in the public sector was being described. But I was tense. That morning, after an all-night session preparing his lengthy statement, H.R. had decided on a massive rewrite of the text he would read and file with the commissioner. With the cheerful assistance of long-serving Dorothy Dee, H.R.'s personal secretary, I organized a corps of typists, each responsible for several pages of amendments. This was long before the days of word processors that amend, shuffle and print text in a few minutes. There was massive retyping to be done.

A platoon of couriers ran several blocks from the Empress

Hotel work rooms to the courthouse and up many steps to avoid the delay of waiting for elevators. I waited at the door of the courtroom at the end of a long hall from the stairway. Behind H.R., who was at a speaker's podium facing Chief Justice Sloan, was a line of M & B executives which extended back to my position — a masterpiece of improvisation not in the textbook of a forester. It was the duty of this line of M & B people to pass forward sheets of text as I received them from the couriers. As H.R. completed reading each page, his left hand moved behind his back to receive the next page.

The system misfired only once, when one of the forwarding executives dropped a page and it fluttered into the aisle in full view of the Chief Justice. The executive, on his hands and knees, slapping at a fluttering paper, caught the eyes of the Chief Justice, who gazed in wonder.

H.R., in perfect composure, said, "Do not worry, your honour, one of my men appears to have lost at least one of his marbles."

"Does he need your help?" asked the commissioner.

"No. I find it better to let him find it. He is an experienced expert," said H.R. in full and proper court language.

I was proud to be one of the first second-generation foresters to formulate a forest management plan and have financial accountability for it. Unfortunately, other factors were at play. Chief among them was the Tree Farm Licence system, which was changing forest management in BC even at that early date. H.R.'s last public effort was to oppose strenuously this approach to forest tenure. Helping him make his presentation was one of my final responsibilities at M & B.

CHAPTER 12

The Tree Farm
Licence is Opposed

E arly in 1955, I was busy in the field supervising MacMillan Bloedel's plantation and thinning operations when I was asked to draft a statement for the company's presentation to the Royal Commission on Forestry. The request was for a bland statement on forest land use that would avoid controversial areas. Shortly thereafter, several major companies published a statement that infuriated MacMillan. At this time, he was in his seventies and in the process of easing himself out of leadership of the company. This fired him up for one final public stand on BC forest policy.

He took over my draft, commandeered a team of M & B staff and set to work. For months my weekends were spent on his boat, the *Marijean*, or at his home at Qualicum Beach discussing M & B's strategy. After one particularly long weekend, H.R. rewarded me with three quarts of fresh, warm milk from his dairy farm. As a boy I had milked a couple of cows every day and enjoyed fresh milk. I took it home as a peace offering to my wife, but she was so angry that my weekends with the kids had

153

been preempted by H.R., that the milk was never used and went sour. Happily, our marriage survived.

The atmosphere through much of Chief Justice Sloan's second royal commission was heavily influenced by the uproar surrounding awarding of Tree Farm Licences. Although one of the main reasons for the existence of the commission was to examine the TFL system, few thorough critiques of it were offered. The notable exception was MacMillan's brief. In many respects the commission hinged on the debate between MacMillan and C.D. Orchard, whose primary contribution was to defend the TFLs.

A deep ideological conflict quickly became visible between these two prominent men. Ironically, Orchard, the public servant and chief forester, spoke for the selfish interests of big industry, while MacMillan, the arch-industrialist, was a staunch defender of small business and a protector of public property.

Chauncey D. Orchard entered the world in New Brunswick on September 25, 1893, "in a farming district without even a crossroads store as a nucleus." When he was four years of age, his family moved to Fredericton. By age eighteen he had completed normal school and obtained his first job as a teacher in a one-room school which had five pupils. Although he left the profession early, from then on he claimed experience as a "school principal."

After Orchard quit teaching, he spent a season roaming New Brunswick on a bicycle, camera in hand, earning spending money by selling photographs of backwood scenes. He then got a government job on a survey crew estimating timber volumes. Among the young men he met was J. Miles Gibson, who would become a distinguished dean of forestry at the University of New Brunswick. Orchard attached himself to Gibson and registered in forestry at UNB, on a schedule that included graduation in the spring of 1916. In late 1914, when Orchard had completed one and a half semesters, Gibson led the entire class to enlist for World War I duty.

On demobilization in May 1919, he returned to UNB for a term that ended in May 1920.

> With graduation imminent the matter of employment became a matter of concern. Forestry was becoming of more public interest and "returned" men were favoured. British Columbia had organized a Forest Service in 1912 and had lost most of their men during the war and now were recruiting staff. The pay, $150 per month, was excellent, and a forester certainly should see the great Pacific coast forests. I applied for, and got, an appointment to the staff of the BC Forest Service.

Orchard graduated on May 3, 1920. The following Saturday, he left Fredericton for Victoria with J.M. Gibson. They were joined en route by C.L. Armstrong, another 1920 graduate. After a leisurely sightseeing trip across Canada, the three men reported to the Forest Branch in Victoria.

J. Miles Gibson was a friendly, outgoing man; even in youth he had a fatherly character and an engaging smile. He was greatly admired by H.R. MacMillan, who employed him as a consultant from time to time, including the occasion on which he asked for Gibson's expert testimony in criticizing Orchard's Tree Farm Licence plan. When Gibson expressed reservations about the Tree Farm Licence, the long relationship between Orchard and Gibson ended.

Harvey Reginald MacMillan was born on September 9, 1885. His father, John Alfred MacMillan, was a local government employee in a Quaker community near Newmarket, Ontario. He died two years after his son and only child arrived. The widow raised her son and helped pay for his schooling by working as a domestic servant. H.R., as he would be called by those close to him in his adult life, lived with his grandfather, a west Scotland immigrant, and his grandmother, whose ancestors had left Scotland for the USA and had then come to Canada as Empire Loyalists.

Describing his early life, MacMillan once said:

> My mother worked as a housekeeper for four dollars per month in order to keep me. That is pretty hard to believe, but it is a fact. It did me a lot of good to see things and understand them. I got an education by her efforts, and stimulated by her efforts I worked myself. I started to work when I was about eleven years old, nights, mornings and all holidays.

As a boy he was a voracious reader of history and biographies of great men such as Alexander Mackenzie, the first European to cross Canada to the Pacific by land. As a scholar, H.R. was outstanding. As an adult he had a style of speaking and writing that was incisive and masterful. When determined to impress an audience such as a royal commissioner examining forestry, he could rise to the same level of drama and dedication to a cause as Winston Churchill.

MacMillan graduated from the Guelph Agricultural College with an honours degree in biology and a bachelor of science. He worked summers in Ontario's Department of Resources, tending tree nurseries and mapping and cruising timber. The autumn after graduation he registered at Yale University, aiming at a bachelor of science in forestry. In March 1907, while still an undergraduate, he obtained a leave of absence and signed on to do his first commercial work in forestry. A syndicate of industrialists from Lindsay, Ontario, hired him to go to BC to stake timber licences. Once he had completed his work with distinction and significant income, he graduated in 1909. Professor Henry S. Graves, later chief of the US Forest Service, rated him one of the most brilliant forestry students to attend Yale.

Once available to the work force, MacMillan was offered

employment as a professor of forestry at the University of New Brunswick, where in a few years he might have had C.D. Orchard as a student. He was also offered a teaching post in Salem, Oregon, but he chose employment in the Forest Service in Ottawa. Posted to the western provinces, he plunged into work — the work that cost him one lung and nearly his life as well.

In 1912, shortly after MacMillan was engaged to organize the BC Forest Service as the first chief forester, he met Martin Allerdale Grainger, author of the Forest Act of 1912 and, some people believe, the man who wrote the royal commission report of that period which recommended creation of the Forest Service. Of all the men H.R. MacMillan met and worked with in a wide-ranging career, he viewed Grainger as one of the greatest.

Grainger was an unusual man. A graduate of Cambridge University with honours in mathematics, he travelled the world intent on seeing the back country, away from the cities. His travels took him to Australia, Yukon and loggers' "float camps" in the coastal fiords of British Columbia. He suffered frost-damaged feet and ever after he wore moccasins. How he arrived in Victoria is unclear. Reportedly to finance his marriage, he wrote a book entitled *Woodsmen of the West*, published in 1908. It was dedicated "To my creditors. . . Affectionately."

In 1952, MacMillan sent Orchard a copy of this book inscribed by Grainger for presentation to W.R. Ross, the minister of lands and forests who had authorized the royal commission report of 1910. MacMillan wrote:

> Under separate cover today I am sending you a copy of *Woodsmen of the West* inscribed by M.A. Grainger for Honourable W.R. Ross. I feel that this particular copy should be in the library of the chief forester.
>
> There probably would have been no "Forest Act" in 1911 if it had not been for the flaming zeal of Grainger.

Any Forest Act prepared without Grainger's zeal would have been like much other legislation — an ineffective dead letter.

Grainger worked night and day for two or three years preparing the report of the royal commission, putting ideas and words into the mouths of commissioners, persuading government to employ Overton Price to bring in the best American thought and experience, searching out all relevant legislation and administration policies of the day, from all of which he drafted the "Forest Act" with Overton Price's help.

It was extraordinary coincidence that he found in the minister of Forests of that period, W.R. Ross, a unique ally, who had been born and raised in the north, who was full of ideals for the country, and whose imagination was stirred and supported by Grainger.

Grainger wrote Ross' speeches and pushed Ross much further than the latter realized. It was Grainger's strength of character that got the Forest Act passed. The government gave wide powers to a technical administrative staff years ahead of any other part of Canada. By passage of the Forest Act, and appointment of a technical staff, the administration of forests was taken out of the hands of the local politicians before they knew it. When those gentlemen woke up, there was nothing they could do about it.

By standing up against the politicians in the East and West Kootenays and in the Fraser Valley and coast district, the minister sacrificed his own political support and came into collision with the "hardboiled" politicians of the government. He would not have done this if it had not been for Grainger.

If the minister had not stood up so strongly for the "Forest Act," and the chief forester during the years 1912 to 1914, the Forest Service would not have taken root.

Orchard arrived in 1920 to join the British Columbia Forest Service. By that time, after serving in the first World War timber supply agency, H.R. had become an exporter of lumber with the creation of the H.R. MacMillan Export Company Limited. Until Orchard became chief forester, it is unlikely that MacMillan, who was then serving as wartime timber controller, had discussed forest policy with Orchard, or even met him. Orchard was a recluse. In temperament, energy and approach to forest management the two men were opposites, to the extent that they repelled rather than attracted each other.

Orchard's career in the BC Forest Service began when he moved somewhat inconclusively about in part-time postings in the interior. By the mid-1920s he was spending considerable time dealing with forest surveys in remote areas. Then, about 1926, Orchard passed surveys over to F.D. Mulholland, who went on to become the father of modern air survey.

Until 1930, Orchard was district forester in Prince George, dealing with twenty-five to thirty bushmills cutting about a hundred million board feet a year. A practising Liberal, he was not popular with local Conservative political officials. When the Liberals came to power, he was transferred to Victoria. There he became assistant forester, Operations Division, replacing Gibson, who had become dean of forestry at UNB.

Operations in Victoria dealt with personnel, preparation of requests for money from the legislature, public relations and many loose ends. Only a person with a bureaucratic, close-to-the-vest mode could be happy in such work. Orchard was comfortable because by instinct and political affiliation he was a Liberal. The depression had clamped a heavy hand on BC. In those days, only the senior men in the Forest Service had civil service appointments. The surveyors, assistant rangers, patrolmen and clerks were appointed by the political bosses in the hinterland and were sacrificed every time the government changed. Orchard, as a paper pusher with acquired skill as a bureaucrat, did excellent work in Operations. He had the ear of the political bosses and could find ways to manage the chaotic staff turnover. Also, in discreet ways, he ensured termination of field staff whom he disliked, and he disliked many people.

In 1936 the chief forester, P.Z. Caverhill, died and was succeeded by E.C. Manning. He knew Orchard could be relied on to deal with political forces, and appointed him assistant chief forester. Manning concentrated on dedicating parks to save forests from commercial harvest, leaving most other matters to Orchard. Late in the decade, as the economy brightened and the country went to war, Orchard's allegiance and talents for shuffling paper were appreciated by the Liberal-controlled legislature.

When H.R. MacMillan joined the war effort as timber supply controller for Canada, he requested and obtained Manning's appointment as British Columbia controller. Orchard temporarily filled the vacant chief forester's chair in Victoria. On February 6, 1941, Manning was killed in Air Canada's first fatal crash, and Orchard was confirmed in the position he occupied. A. Wells Gray, a long-time Liberal party follower, was the minister of lands and forests and John Hart headed a Liberal-Conservative coalition.

The stage was set for Orchard to create the Tree Farm Licence system that would soon plunge the industry into controversy. The second Sloan Commission, ordered by W.A.C. Bennett, was an attempt at damage control for the uproar surrounding TFLs. Orchard had sowed a hurricane and now had to reap it, as the second royal commission prepared to examine the events he had set in motion.

Sloan started slowly with sympathetic questioning of Orchard as the chief spokesman for the Forest Service. Orchard defended his tenure system against all critics. At the same time, he told the commission that the Forest Service had been forced to fight pressure from parts of industry that wanted to regulate competition out of existence. He said the regulation had been requested to uphold a variety of industry sections, including minority groups, certain classes of operators or types of operations, and industries in particular regions.

> The small seeking protection from the big. The established seeking protection from the newcomers. The pole operators from the sawlog operators. The "big" very much in quotation marks. I don't know what's big and what's small. The "big" to be forced to insure the continued existence or even the profit of the "small." And all these things have been urged on us, and if we had yielded, we would have been regulating today every move and turn the industry made.

Orchard commented that the imposition of his new system had inevitably and unavoidably led to doubts, criticism and active opposition by some parties. He described the early applications as containing some anomalies and pieces of "fuzzy" administration. This was Orchard's description of a process which, over the previous seven or eight years, had seen the creation of some monstrously large Tree Farm Licences, in violation of every principle he had tried to enshrine in the system. The term "fuzzy" also failed to describe the bribery and corruption of which he as chief forester had knowledge. Yet he went on to advocate a further extension of the Tree Farm Licence system.

After David Sturdy's submission to the inquiry was refused, the hearings took on the character of a criminal trial. Those in favour of Tree Farm Licences were treated as persons of great wisdom, while critics were subjected to exhaustive cross-examination, not just on their documents and their opinions, but on their motives. As a result, little time was spent on substance.

H.R. MacMillan's testimony is a case in point. He was a forester of distinction, had been the first chief forester of British Columbia and was an organizer of the Forest Service. By the time the commission was ordered, H.R. had been a leading industrialist for nearly forty-five years. As head of a major company, he controlled one of the largest acreages of privately owned forest land in all of Canada. MacMillan's land was under crop-replacing silviculture and, thus, intensive sustained yield management. His professional knowledge of forest management was unparalleled, and he submitted much material and supported it with authoritative statistics. Every line of his testimony was subjected to cross-examination, all of which concentrated on his motives for opposing the Tree Farm Licence concept.

One can only speculate why the chief justice permitted this type of grilling. MacMillan was most vociferously opposed by Orchard, who was protecting his creation, and those companies seeking Tree Farm Licences in the overcut Vancouver Forest District. Their allegation was that MacMillan wanted to solidify his dominance in the Vancouver Forest District by excluding all other companies. The chief justice seemed to go along with this, in spite of MacMillan's stated willingness to withdraw M & B's new TFL applications and compete equally for timber in a open log market.

At the opening of the commission inquiry, about twelve Tree Farm Licences had been issued in the Vancouver Forest District, several in the Prince Rupert District and several smaller ones in the vast underdeveloped interior forest. There were applications approved, in principle, for almost all of the public timber in the Vancouver District. If they were issued, the smaller independent log producers supplying sawmills which bought on the open market would be displaced. This would impair survival of coastal log-buying manufacturing units. M & B had two relatively small Tree Farm Licences on which lands contributed by the company formed a significant portion of the licences.

MacMillan's position was that no further Tree Farm Licences should be issued in the inner coastal area of the Vancouver Forest District. By taking this position, he was denying his own company another licence in this significant forest area. His opponents did not cross-examine him on that point. Instead, they attempted to portray him as a self-centred, greedy industrialist, already in control of too much timber and determined to keep his competitors weak.

Because Sloan rejected MacMillan's recommendations, and did not record them as an alternative in the commission report, the government was able to ignore MacMillan's wisdom.

In 1956, the processing component of the interior forest industry consisted of small bushmills making low-quality lumber and selling into an uncertain market. The economic centre of the industry was the Vancouver Forest District. It was in this district that the pressure and shortcomings of timber allocation were visible. They needed to be solved, both in terms of the public interest and certainly in terms of wise use of the forest. MacMillan addressed himself to these issues. He argued forcefully that the solution to the looming problems of the Vancouver district was not to create more Tree Farm Licences, but to continue allocating competitive timber sales to the independent logging sector. This would create a viable log market to supply the independent sawmills. It would also allow the Forest Service to start large-scale silviculture on lands outside the TFLs. The vigour and depth of his logic surprised Chief Justice Sloan and, most particularly, MacMillan's business rivals. They thought that as a leading industrialist he had "lost his marbles" to utter such heresies, and they tried to discredit his statements as the ramblings of a senile old man.

"Great effort is justified," he said, "to accomplish the objective of bringing the sustained yield of the Vancouver Forest District up to the present annual cut, thereby avoiding closing mills and reducing employment. . . . This ten million acres of forest produced in 1955 about seventy percent of British Columbia's 1955 total of forest products. . . and it is the greatest single factor in supporting the people of this province. . . . We are confident that the present overcut of the Vancouver Forest District can be corrected, within a reasonable number of years, without putting any operators out of business or men out of work."

MacMillan then went on to list the detailed steps needed to bring about sustained yield in the district. A suitable period within which to do the job, say thirty years, should be chosen. The lands not satisfactorily restocked, about a million acres of public land and another half million acres of private lands, should be reforested in the first twenty years. Today, thirty-five years after the powers that be ignored MacMillan's advice, there are now about two million acres of land not satisfactorily restocked in the Vancouver forest region.

MacMillan also advocated better recovery of waste on logging sites: "Even the best operators can afford to log still cleaner than at present," he told Sloan. In those days, only logs with tops 12 inches and larger had to be harvested. Close use logging standards did not become mandatory for another twelve years. Even through most of the 1980s these standards were relaxed by the Forest Service on the instructions of its political masters, in order to increase the revenues of the monopoly that has taken over most of the cutting rights in the Vancouver region. This practice, in the double-speak of the fixers, was called "sympathetic administration."

Further, H.R. said, steps should be taken to reduce the export of logs and chips. Combined with the fuller use of sawmill wood waste in pulp mills, this would reduce the use of logs in pulp mills and, consequently, decrease the area logged each year, stretching out the timber supply and lowering reforestation costs.

After describing what should be done in the district, MacMillan went on to counter the arguments of those advocating more Tree Farm Licences in the area. First, he dealt with the proposition that the Forest Service was unable to manage the lands and that, therefore, they would be better managed in Tree Farm Licences.

In the Vancouver Forest District, the selection of
public forests cannot be given to a few applicants without depriving, to the extent of the forest thus taken out
of circulation, all the many hundreds of other operators
in the region. . . . We cannot accept the applied inability
of the Forest Service [as stated earlier in the commission
hearings by Orchard] to bring about forest management
on Public Working Circles [the lands outside Tree Farm
Licences]. The forests in Public Working Circles can be
as well managed as can forests in any [Tree Farm]
Licence. All you have to do is employ enough men of
the same calibre and spend as much money and there is
then no earthly reason why you cannot get as good
results.

MacMillan said that Orchard would "be surprised at the
results he could obtain if he spent as much money and employed
as many men in Public Working Circles as the licencees are
required by his own administration to employ in their [Tree
Farm] Licences."

Next, MacMillan defended the free market and competitive
forest industry, against those who wanted to give or get timber
without having to bid for it.

A lot of effort has been spent and time taken up during
the sittings of this commission in an effort to persuade
you, Mr. Commissioner, to a conclusion that public
timber should be parcelled out to the selected few,
selected on one basis or another, but all with the sole
objective that the few should survive and the many
struggle for their existence until they can struggle no
more and cease to trouble. To this we are unalterably
opposed.

The public forests are public property and one citizen

has just as much right as another to bring it into productivity and make money doing it if he can. The principle is as old as the French Revolution — there is nothing novel about it — there is no God-given right in any man to say who shall and who shall not enjoy the benefits of public property. Why should there be some closed circle applied to the public forest in Vancouver District where the demand for wood is already greater than the supply?...Timber sales should be open to anyone.... There is nothing peculiar about this. It is a Canadian concept on which this country has been built and run...and I for one can see no good reason why we should at this late date cast aside our heritage for the mid-European concept of the managed state.

Mr. Bentley of Canadian Forest Products, who would expel those he classifies as "inefficient" operators, would thus have all industry frozen at its present level — a convenient level at which to freeze as far as he is concerned — but one which he would have been first to complain had that step been advocated twenty years ago [when he immigrated to this country].

Mr. Wismer [a lawyer representing a consortium of sawmills] has fought strenuously for the granting of a number of [Tree Farm Licences] covering a vast acreage in this congested Vancouver Forest District on the plea that they are for existing industries which should be kept alive in perpetuity. Why, one cannot see. It is urged that one of these companies is entitled to that preservation because it started in the forest industry in 1893....By what right does this handful of operators claim that they should be relieved of the perils of competition and flagging energy?...

In the long history of this forest district few mills have depended for their wood supply solely upon the forests they own. The alert operator kept himself in business and succeeded by seeking out and acquiring in open competition, stands of public timber which served his purpose. No change has yet taken place which would prevent the continuation of that process. Our present economy will survive so long as, but only if, the Crown forests in this Vancouver Forest District can be reached and acquired by the hundreds of operators who earn their livelihoods from this land and play their part in our economic life. . . . The inefficient will drop out — competition has always tended to eliminate the inefficient and to reward the efficient. No man should say, be he private citizen or public servant, this man shall be allowed to continue, that man shall drop out. . . .

No bonus in the form of a [Tree Farm Licence] need be expended by the public to start anyone else in business in this district. No timber bonus should be given to keep in business a few of those who now are here. Those who urge the contrary do so in fear of the fate which may be in store for them if they fail to maintain their efficiency and bear the brunt of the competition of their peers. They look upon this commission as a Heaven-sent opportunity to enable them to take a tow instead of continuing to work their passage. They want to be awarded all the timber they could ever need even though the results will be that the timber available for their present competitors will be correspondingly reduced. Other wood consumers less powerful, less crafty, but who are equally good Canadians, will be put out of business.

MacMillan made two appearances before Sloan over a period of several days. Following his testimony, he was grilled for days, particularly by lawyers for the commission and the major companies who were seeking more Tree Farm Licences in the disputed Vancouver District. In summing up for the commissioner, MacMillan spoke to the public and future generations. He stressed that the remaining timber in the district "should be sold at fair market price as determined in a competitive open log market as a means of ensuring the public treasury receives full value for the timber it sells to industrial users."

In his earlier submission, MacMillan had expressed his belief in the value to the province of the independent loggers who were being forced out by the Tree Farm Licences.

> It will be a sorry day for. . . British Columbia when the forest industry here consists chiefly of a very few big companies, holding most of the good timber — or pretty near all of it — and good growing sites to the disadvantage and early extermination of the most hard working, virile, versatile, and ingenious element of our population, the independent market logger and the small mill man . . .
>
> By "independent market logger" we mean the logger who is free to make his important business decisions. He is an experienced man and has some capital, often mostly in the form of machinery. He is free to purchase timber, wherever he may find it available, by government timber sale or elsewhere, or to seek logging contracts on privately-owned timber. He decides how he will open up his show and the size of his operation. He makes his own choice as to whom he will buy from, sell to, join in a contract, or if he will operate as a contractor [on a TFL]. If he borrows money, he chooses the lender, and is not under duress in accepting the lender's terms. He owns his logs and does not have to agree to sell them below the market price as an usurious condition of getting a loan or being allowed the chance to go logging. If he makes a profit it is his. If he makes a loss, he survives or goes into liquidation.
>
> There is every reason to avoid legislating or regulat-

ing the market logger out of existence.... There is no
apparent good and sufficient reason why any of the large
companies should be aided by government politics to
grow bigger at the expense of the smaller. Our forest
industry is healthier if it consists of as many independent
units as can be supported.

In cross-examination, H.R.'s detractors tried to undermine
the importance of the small, independent sector, and MacM-
illan came back again and again in their defence. It is sadly
ironic that in the years since he made these statements, Mac-
Millan has so often been portrayed as the archetypal big business tycoon. In fact, as the transcript of the commission reveals,
he was probably the most articulate spokesman for the small
business community. H.R.'s concern for these people went
beyond the mere preservation of a certain business sector:

> The lives of three-quarters of those communities de-
> pends on independent operators... and it's a powerful
> argument with me in thinking about this problem that
> British Columbia will be a much more healthy place if
> we can keep all these communities, and more like them,
> going, inhabited by people who are independently run-
> ning their own business, on no matter how small a scale.

More than once, MacMillan delivered a warning.

> The division of this vast and important industry into
> two groups, on the one hand a few large units protected
> partially or fully for raw material by [Tree Farm Li-
> cences], and on the other hand a thousand or more
> smaller units who already see the end of the timber
> available to them, would furnish the motive for drastic
> political overturn.

He made a dramatic prediction:

> A few companies would acquire control of resources and form a monopoly. It will be managed by professional bureaucrats, fixers with a penthouse viewpoint who, never having had rain in their lunch buckets, would abuse the forest. Public interest would be victimized because the citizen business needed to provide the efficiency of competition would be denied logs and thereby be prevented from penetration of the market.

But MacMillan's advice was ignored. Such a monopoly has formed, and penetrates all aspects of forestry. It controls the Forest Service and, in the back rooms of power, imposes its wishes on government in a way that damages the interests of the public. The monopoly has awesome power as it feasts off the public heritage.

To my knowledge there has never been a royal commission so critical to the public interest, that has omitted evidence so essential to protecting that interest. MacMillan isolated each of the flaws in Orchard's concept and predicted the disaster that would occur if changes were not made. His arguments against further allocations of TFLs in the Vancouver district foresaw the inequities, injustices and poor forest management practices the TFL system would inflict on the province for the next half century. MacMillan's predictions of thirty-five years ago are still remarkable for their prophetic accuracy. They underline the need for corrective action to turn the present sorry state of forest policy in British Columbia in a positive direction.

CHAPTER 13

The Best Use of Timber

One Saturday morning in the late 1950s, my home telephone rang well before breakfast time. My wife answered, listened a moment and said, "Stop joking. It is too early." The receiver was returned with undue force.

"Some joker," she reported, "says he is H.R. MacMillan and wants to talk to you."

Before I could respond, the bell rang again. "Sorry to upset your wife," said H.R., "but I'd like to look at some forest areas." He said he would pick me up by eight o'clock. "And bring your rifle," he added, "we might see a deer or two."

By mid-morning, I was crouched on a hillside with the sun at my back, dressing a two-pronged buck. H.R. sat on a stump munching a sandwich. Out of the corner of my eye, I thought I saw him brush a tear from his cheek. My father, also seventy-four years of age at the time, would often weep silently when overtired or emotionally drained. I continued with the deer but from time to time glanced at H.R. Moments later, I knew he was in trouble.

"H.R., are you feeling ill?" I asked.

"No," was the abrupt reply.

I finished my work, then sat beside H.R. on the stump. There was no question about it: tears stood on his cheeks. On the logged-off hillside across the valley, ten-year-old plantation seedlings, uniformly spaced with crowns well above the stumps of the old forest, glittered with vitality. Farther up the same hillside, natural regeneration, nearly twenty years old, the product of a lightning fire, shone in healthy vigour. It had been thinned by my crews so that the trees would have optimum space for growth. This was tree farming, and was one of the first British Columbia silviculture projects paid for by corporate funding, defined and approved as commercial forestry, as distinct from research.

"Excellent work," said MacMillan. Then, wiping his eyes to get his emotions under control, he continued. "Ian! Remember my words. When the pulp and paper people get a hold of my company it will be like a blight on the prairie wheat."

I exclaimed in surprise. "I thought they were good people," I told him, "that as engineers and trained executives they would make the company prosperous."

H.R. shook his head and his heavy eyebrows moved back and forth in a half circle. "No! They do not understand the forest and they will waste and abuse the very foundation of the company."

I silently wondered if these were the musings of an old man with a mind dwelling only on past achievements. I wondered if this statement had come from the same considered judgment that years before had formed a plan, set a goal and moved step by step to achieve it. For the rest of the day, deer hunting was forgotten. We were two foresters driving through the lowland country, a deceased two-pronged buck wrapped in a canvas in the trunk of the Rolls Royce. We inspected new forests growing on the sites of former railway logging operations, and talked for hours about the production and market strategies needed if the company and the province were to prosper.

MacMillan said that we must make the best economic use of all the components of the forest. We need modernized big-log mills that make the best of high-grade, specialty lumber. For small-log mills producing structural lumber, we need thin kerf head saw technology, with pre-sorted logs moving past the saw, nose to tail in linear flow. We have enough back-and-forth, stop-and-go, old-fashioned head rigs. They must be abandoned so we can make precision-sawn wood with smooth surfaces. Then we do not have to spend money passing lumber through a planer to get the size uniformity the customer demands. We will have to return to drying lumber in kilns. Green lumber, particularly hemlock and balsam that is stained with mold, will not command a proper price. It may not even sell, in markets where there is the opportunity to get precision-sawn, dry lumber like Europeans produce from their forests and Americans will produce from their pine stands in the former cotton belt. We have to increase our productivity to a level where we can afford the wages our people will demand. We must increase productivity if we are going to compete in world markets supplied by workmen who are at least as clever, at least as dedicated and very much closer to the marketplace than we in our remote location in the north Pacific.

H.R. then mused on what he expected the pulp and paper people would do: "They are instinctive monopolists," he said, "and are not content to rely upon sawmill chips for their furnish. They want first class, whole logs to pour through chippers at high speed. For that they will misuse the existing forest and cut the new forest before it is ready for a proper harvest. They will ignore profits available in the lumber and plywood markets," he went on, "and will neglect to provide capital for new technology and improved efficiency in our sawmills and plywood factories. When they gain control of the forest, acting as a monopoly and fixing prices, which is the way the pulp and paper people prefer to do business, they will deny access to those who would invest in modernized sawmill technology and those with the entrepreneurial fortitude to compete for business.

"The pulp people, in concert with politicians, will frustrate entrepreneurs and deny them access to public forests. In due course the mismanagement of neglect will be the excuse for the pulp and paper people to vacate the solid wood product markets and divert more and more attention to pulp and paper. Broad diversification, which is the fundamental strength of MacMillan Bloedel, will be abandoned by executives with a pulp-and-paper mindset. They will wander far and wide, grasping for a position in consumer markets and enterprises they do not understand. The more they high-grade easy profits by selecting the areas that can be logged at the lowest cost and the best species in the forests, the more they waste the resource, the more they neglect silviculture, and the more they abuse their neighbours and citizens who own the forest, the greater will be the lost prestige, denied good will and declined profitability of the company. It is that road the pulp and paper people will travel.

"They do not understand the forest," he said. "It is obscured by egos warped by chemicals, smells and the arrogance attached to mega-dollar investments. When foresters do not have a strong role in planning and decision making in a forest industry company then there will be dark days in British Columbia."

One of my major tasks at M & B was to transform the practices and attitudes of a company built over half a century of railway logging. These attitudes failed to recognize the value of the forest resources and led to waste in the woods and a misuse of logs in the mill, all in the name of faster and easier revenues. I ran into some difficulty introducing sanity into the use of timber in M & B, and if it had not been for MacMillan's full support, the policy would have failed.

One central problem was the basis of measuring logs — scaling. We did not measure the solid wood content in a log. Instead, we calculated the amount of lumber we could produce from it. This method wildly distorts the calculation of timber in the forest and has no relevance in sustained yield crop measurement.

In the late 1700s, solid wood measure was used in England and Europe with no deductions for sawdust and other waste incurred in the manufacture of lumber. The first known lumber content scale was published in Troy, New York, in 1805 by a sawmiller. It was soon introduced in every timber area in the US and Canada. Every local jurisdiction developed its own distinctive "Scale Rule." All were subjective and irrational, created to overstate the amount of wood lost in sawdust, trim and edgings so that the purchaser of timber would always have an overrun. The owner of the trees was forced to bear the waste of solid wood and, in the end, he was defrauded. This system worked particularly well in publicly owned forests where politicians could be persuaded to implement it.

British Columbia, at the end of the nineteenth century, was the last frontier for lumbermen to exploit as they moved west. They created a BC log scale with the highest waste of solid wood and, thus, the least scale of lumber content in North America. This scale favoured the sawmiller and short-changed the public in payment for timber, called stumpage. A treatise published in 1906 by Henry Solon Graves, chief forester for the US Department of Agriculture, examined forty-five lumber scale rules in use in North America, including the BC scale. Not too surprisingly, the BC scale included some of the lowest measurements of lumber content. In comparison, a scale known as the International Rule included some of the highest measurements.

The International Rule was developed by Judson F. Clark when he worked at the Ontario Department of Lands and Forests in 1906. His rule was derived from detailed sawmill output measurements, both in BC and in eastern Canada. It is the most accurate of all the many lumber rules in use in North America — which is to say, it is the most honest in terms of the relationship between actual log size and lumber content. On the other hand, the BC rule was one of the most dishonest, particularly in measuring the big west coast logs that were commonly cut into huge cants. These twelve- or even twenty-four-inch square cants produced little waste relative to the one-inch boards on which the BC scaling system was based. In BC the sawmillers who authored the log scale rule displayed the genius of bank robbers. They devised a system that determined the lowest lumber content of all the major scale rules in use, and it was committed to law by politicians who were paid tribute by early sawmillers.

The failure to use a solid wood scaling system in the allocation of Tree Farm Licences and in the calculation of allowable annual harvests brought foresters into the business of distorted timber volumes. They soon lost any accurate sense of measurement as applied to forest inventories, rates of annual growth, actual volumes harvested and other statistics essential to the maintenance of economic health. The BC Forest Service adopted solid wood measure nearly twenty years after Orchard proposed his Tree Farm Licence, which means that all the planning, dialogue and policy considerations were based on a flawed measure.

This was the situation during both Sloan Royal Commissions. In about 1960, it was discovered that the first thirty or so Tree Farm Licences had been allocated much more public timber, measured in solid wood content, than intended. There was no public admission of this fact until Peter Pearse published his royal commission report in 1976.

The political response to this excessive allocation was to instruct the TFL holders to "use it or lose it." The industry responded in a variety of subtle and occasionally not-so-subtle ways to render the over-allocation meaningless, and devised ways to waste the less profitable solid wood. One method was to store logs in water for prolonged periods prior to scaling, so that unwanted species and grades of logs were disposed of. This practice was innovative, but deceitful. With an emerging pulp industry consuming logs measured in lumber scale, the cost of production and profit generation became fictions leading to irrational production management decisions.

In his memoirs, Orchard recounts the history of the more honest solid wood, cubic content scale which took such a long time to be adopted by BC. According to Orchard, cubic scale was written into forestry law in 1944, but was withdrawn during first reading in the legislature. This was because industry had spent plenty of money lobbying it out of statute. Cubic scale was again written into law in 1946, but was defined as an elective of industry. Finally, in 1952, the Social Credit government ordered discontinuation of board foot scale. They did so, however, without consulting the Forest Service, and Orchard was outraged at their high-handed action. Instead of supporting his minister, Orchard waffled, and pressure from the industry caused the government to capitulate one more time. It was not until Ray Williston took charge that cubic scale became the measurement base.

When I joined M & B in 1951, the company's pulp division was forging ahead, intent on consuming logs. The original design of the Harmac pulp mill included and actually started operation of a drum barker. It would consume cord wood purchased from land owners who would be slashing down twenty- to thirty-year-old growing stock from new forests. These owners were to be paid using a flawed scale, which would be a deception that amounted to theft of their property. At the same time, logging slash on company land, representing a solid wood volume of about 30 percent of the crop, was being burned at great expense and risk to the surrounding forests. The pulp management people wanted the luxury of buying the wood based on lumber scale. I insisted that they must at least pay based on solid wood scale, not lumber scale.

This created an impasse that had to be resolved by the Forestry and Timber Committee. I knew that MacMillan, Bloedel and Van Dusen, who had all spent their lives dealing in lumber scale, would be unlikely to want to deal in solid wood measure. I decided to put something simple in front of them.

An examination of the log supply department's accounting procedures showed how distortions occurred. All cost records were in board feet lumber scale. This method indicated that the company's North West Bay division was a high-cost logging division making a narrow profit margin. But a series of calculations showed this was a delusion created by the faulty measure of timber. Measured in solid wood, North West Bay produced at the lowest cost. Thus, in terms of fibre produced for pulp mill use, North West Bay contributed the greatest profit of any logging division. Of course this analysis did not look so good on the pulp mill's books, but it was a corporate profit stemming from the best use of timber and that was what counted. The debate was short, and with great rapidity all costing of silviculture and forestry expenditures were converted to solid measure. Likewise, profit generation in all manufacturing was measured in relation to solid wood consumed. With that decision, the buying and selling of logs became a tool in determining the best use of the corporation's forest assets.

So it was that M & B moved to a co-ordinated and well-disciplined reforestation program early in the 1950s. The paramount reason was the existence of a senior committee of directors who met every month to scrutinize, approve and seek the best economic use of corporate-owned timber.

In the period between 1960 and 1978, after the departure of H.R., Hoffmeister and others who had understood the value of the company's forests, the blight was indeed on the prairie wheat. It spread at a dizzying pace through the affairs of the company. Senior management turned their backs on the forest and the wood product business to lurch about the world dabbling in venture capital financing, building aircraft and speculating in real estate and the ship charter business.

In time, the Vancouver headquarters of the company became an establishment of lawyers, accountants and pulp and paper thinkers who did not know the forest. There are many stories, all painful, all ridiculous and, unfortunately, all true. One senior executive refusing to speak to another for several years. Other executives refusing to sit with another present in the same meeting. A pro forma senior executive stripped of authority, allowed to use his office as a retreat from the real world. Petty, silly internal struggles spread shadowy tentacles of tension to lower floors and into field operations. The forest was all but forgotten. The best and easiest timber was highgraded. Waste in the slash rose to appalling levels. The cost of log production became unconscionable. The eyes of the executives were so far from the forest that a junior employee managed to steal a multi-million-dollar volume of company-produced logs over a period of years, and the crime was discovered by people outside the company.

The heart, if not the soul, of the company which had been so judiciously husbanded in former years, was misused for an agonizing decade and a half. In early 1976, information began to leak out that the company's first loss would be reported.

H.R. MacMillan, in his ninety-first year and confined to his home, wrote worried notes to one of M & B's officers requesting information. In a sense, none was needed because H.R., twenty years earlier, had foretold events. He had said, "it will be managed by bureaucrats, fixers with a penthouse viewpoint who, never having had rain in their lunch buckets, would abuse the forest."

When H.R. MacMillan died, the Vancouver *Sun* stated he had once told a friend, "God is very wise. When a man has lived a long time and has learned a great deal about how to do things, God arranges to take him away. It is a good rule." God in his merciful wisdom chose to take H.R. away on February 9, 1976, just a few months before an official 1975 financial statement for MacMillan Bloedel reported a huge loss — the first in the fifty-three-year history of the company — of $18.8 million on a sales income of $1.2 billion. Even the logging operations in the splendid BC forests lost money.

H.R. had deplored technology that wasted timber. In his view, subsidizing the pulp and paper industry with "under-priced chips" obtained from sawmills, while pulp log and small log pulp wood were left as waste in the forest slash, was one cause of the "blight." He was opposed to the selling of sawmill chips at less than the cost of equivalent log content from the forest. He knew that over time this would damage the sawmill industry and waste the small logs in the forest, including silvicultural thinnings available from the new forests. He maintained that the underpricing of raw material because of obsolete, inefficient manufacturing amounted to theft of the usable crop-growing potential. Waste of the mature forest accelerated the rate at which land was cleared, and increased the rate of silvicultural spending on crop replacement. This directly plundered capital invested in forest crops. My job description, on the other hand, expressly stated that I was to practise sustained yield crop production, but that the cost of the new crop was not to be inflated in any way by waste in the woods or in the mills.

M & B's losses due to obsolete sawmills and other technology in 1975, excluding unmeasured damage to the corporate forest property, both owned and under licence, works out to roughly $30 million in the plywood and lumber sectors. That does not take into account the costs of harvesting more timber than would have been necessary had modern manufacturing technology been in place. To the extent that the value of owned timber increases if conserved, the 1975 events, which MacMillan foresaw, wasted a large segment of a hard-won timber asset. If management was prepared to waste the timber crop, it would have been better off buying logs on the open market and conserving the company timber stands, which over time inflate in value.

When Hoffmeister operated MacMillan Bloedel as board chairman, the two most senior committees of directors, Finance and Policy, and Forestry and Timber, included the major shareholders — H.R. MacMillan, Prentice Bloedel and W.J. Van Dusen, with Hoffmeister as chairman. Under Hoffmeister's successor, these committees were either disbanded or made impotent by ad hoc decisions which ignored the forest and overruled accountable executives. It was then that corporate action began to drift, in terms of the best economic use of the precious timber resource. Best use was not a regular topic of discussion; therefore, it was removed as a goal for managers of operating divisions. Silviculture dwindled until it was only a shop window for publicity and public relations, rather than a discipline to sustain corporate equity in timber. This failure to make the best economic use of the forest cost the company income in the manufacturing divisions. Added to that was an immeasurable loss of company timber wasted in the slash, because the pulp and paper sector used lumber and plywood logs instead of using lower grade logs unsuitable for lumber or plywood. The evidence is that about 60 percent of log input to the pulp mills in the period under discussion was prime sawlog material. This was a needless, wasteful liquidation of capital and publicly owned forests.

On that September day at Nanaimo Lakes, H.R. had expressed his professional satisfaction with our silviculture, then wept tears of frustration because he despaired of being able to control the impact of the pulp and paper mindset on his company. At that point, I began to examine my own position as a professional forester at MacMillan Bloedel. By early 1958 Hoffmeister had been replaced by J.V. Clyne, a man who knew little of the forest. I decided to resign and become an entrepreneur. I knew that in M & B's emerging management style, I could not practise my profession as a forester whose primary concern was the forests. By that time, the company, along with the other pulp-dominated holders of Tree Farm Licences, wanted foresters who were chiefly concerned with the short-term financial position of the company. Inevitably, this policy was instituted at the expense of the forests they owned or leased.

There were compelling reasons for me to become my own man and serve my own conscience. I knew that if I could not practise my profession as a forester, I would not be comfortable picking up my monthly paycheque. In fact, I resigned from M & B about a year sooner than I had first intended.

At a reception for management staff, organized for the purpose of introducing Clyne, I experienced an abrupt example of the new chairman's management style. Clyne was being escorted around and introduced to everyone. When my turn came he had a drink in his hand, which he finished before he spoke to me. Then he handed me his empty glass and ordered me to have it refilled. A bar steward, employed for that task, came by and I asked him to get Clyne a refill. In an angry outburst, Clyne addressed me in abusive tones, saying he had asked me to get the drink and I should do so promptly. I gave him a forthright negative response in language that, in my opinion, was appropriate. Before Clyne recovered his composure the bar steward delivered the drink.

The next day, without elaboration, I handed in my resignation to my boss, Ernie Shorter, the executive vice-president of production. Shorter refused to accept it. Instead, he asked me to take several weeks' holiday and reconsider. In deference to him I complied, and on my return, Shorter offered me a promotion to general manager of timber allocation, working as his executive assistant. The first thing he wanted me to do was to go to the Queen Charlotte Islands and write him a report stating that a log dump built there had been a mistake.

"Ernie," I said. "If you want a report of that kind you could write it yourself without going out of the office. If I went up there I might just find that it was a great dump, and that is not want you want."

He looked surprised and admitted he was not prepared to accept my resignation because of his concern about where I might find other employment. Then he told me he had discussed my capabilities with the managers of a pulp mill then under construction near Cranbrook. A job was available for me there, at no reduction in income. I thanked him for his interest and concern, and departed. I was paid by M & B for some months before I received a note from Shorter, in longhand, formally accepting my resignation. I think I may be one of the few people who, when offering his resignation, did not get an order to clear his desk by five o'clock.

Some years later, about 1974, when I was chief executive officer of the Canadian operations of Triangle Pacific Forest Products, and a vice-president and director of the US parent company, my supply and sales office in Vancouver bought about 20 million board feet of lumber per month for resale in the US through Triangle Pacific's docks and lumberyards. A sizeable portion of this was purchased from M & B. I was one of the largest single buyers of M & B lumber for the Atlantic coast trade. One day, at a cocktail party of people in the lumber business, I was surprised to have Jack Clyne personally bring me a drink. He expressed his regret that I had not stayed with his company and said that if I decided to leave my position with Triangle Pacific he would like me to come and talk to him. This event serves to illustrate how few people make up the forest industry business community in Vancouver. In New York, where I had an office for a time, one would not see the same people twice in the course of a month. In Vancouver, one meets the same people every day within two blocks of the office.

Today, looking back on my work as a professional forester, I see a great danger for BC in a policy that allows increased control of public forests by pulp and paper conglomerates. Independent, locally controlled business is being shouldered out of existence, misuse of timber has become a disease and sustained yield forestry is little more than a public relations gesture.

The kind of corporate structure that operates in the pulp and paper industry demonstrates a lack of commitment to BC. These companies reside in highrise towers in distant locations, employing fixers intent on shuffling, prodding and using their economic muscle to gain control of the forest crop. They are delinquent in forest management in BC, while at the same time they are investing in lands in the southern hemisphere to grow pine trees on a fifteen-year rotation. When that is achieved, operations will be phased out in BC. During their passage in this province, they will have displaced independent business, stripped off the easy timber, scarred the mountainsides with huge clear-cuts and carried out crop-replacing silviculture at only a token level. Little will be done to achieve the quality of silviculture implicit in the Magna Carta concept of forestry.

That concept of the forester — as protector of the realm — must be revived as a force to preserve the complex, interdependent ecosystem of British Columbia. The professional forester must come out of the closet and practise his profession, or the blight that H.R. MacMillan foretold will remain and spread.

CHAPTER 14

A Fledgling Entrepreneur

After resigning from M & B, I got together with two partners, R.J. McKercher and J. Grant Williams, and set up a company engaged in logging, road construction and trucking. McKercher, a former employee of M & B, was a graduate forester and a dedicated logger. Grant Williams was an outstanding heavy construction man. As a teen-ager, he had been a tailgunner in a bomber and survived more than sixty raids over Germany, when the life expectancy in those crews was less than ten raids.

In 1961, we bought the assets of a logger who had gone into bankruptcy working on contract to BC Forest Products on TFL 22 at Ucluelet — the same infamous TFL that had sent Bob Sommers to jail. One of our immediate problems was BCFP's requirement that we store loose logs in the harbour. There they would await a log barge that would haul them to Victoria for sorting and scaling in a water-based depot, and we were to be paid for volume after the logs were scaled. Logs were lost in transport, sunk in storage and misplaced so that some were fed into the sawmill without first being scaled. We soon discovered the cause of our predecessor's bankruptcy — nearly 25 percent of his production had been lost, sunk or stolen before it was scaled. Now we were losing money, as was the public treasury.

We took the matter to the company's managers. After an exchange of angry words, the scaling process was transferred to Ucluelet Harbour. Our losses were reduced; they were not eliminated, however, because our employer insisted on delaying the scale until the day before the barge came to load out the water-stored logs. Ucluelet Harbour was littered with hundreds of sunken logs. We attempted to convince the Forest Service that public money was being lost and that storage and scale of logs should be done on land. There was no interest. We then brought in a portable sawmill, set it up in an abandoned aircraft hangar and obtained a lumber order from M & B. We salvaged the logs which had been sunk in the harbour. In an instant, the Forest Service was demanding payment of stumpage and royalty. We refused to pay on the grounds that we were salvaging. If the Forest Service wanted to recover public equity it should order BC Forest Products to establish a dryland log sort where each truckload of logs would be scaled before title passed to the licencee. Only after I had discussed the situation with Forest Minister Ray Williston, did the Forest Service act.

As soon as our logging company was paid in full for the logs we produced, we began making a profit. In those days equipment for a logging side cost perhaps $50,000. The sawmill cost us about $6,000 and made an instant profit, not by cutting lumber but by forcing the Forest Service to scale public property before it was wasted through sinkage. That crude sawmill was one of the best investments we ever made. It forced our employer to get serious about scaling our logs and, after Williston knocked some heads in the Forest Service, the public equity was recovered. Our company, Millstream Timber Limited, was one of the first coastal loggers to achieve scaling on land prior to watering the logs. Our data indicated a previous wastage of about 15 percent of public property due to the failure of the Forest Service.

In the same period, our consulting company, Mahood, Mc-Kercher and Associates, started work in Italy, the Dutch East Indies, Central America and throughout North America, including BC. For a time we bought logs in the Vancouver Log Market, had them sawn under contract with S & R Sawmills at Port Kells, and sold the lumber into the US market. We bought logs left as waste by the big companies — clear cedar slabs, yellow cedar and high grade white pine — and made money because we had no capital invested in logging equipment or sawmills.

Our industrial consulting division, which similarly had no capital invested, did timber appraisals and economic studies for major BC companies. In that capacity I worked closely with Ray Williston, who had rejected the Tree Farm Licence for use in the interior. I helped design the Pulpwood Harvesting Licence which made pulp wood and chips available from sawlog timber sales. The Northwood pulp mill complex at Prince George was the first founded on chips that came from close-use harvest of the forest. The pulp mill at Quesnel was likewise founded on chips supplied by local sawmills. At the time of authorization, it was prohibited from using sawlogs. Pulp was now being manufactured from wood otherwise burned in beehive burners or disposed of in landfills.

In 1961, when the Council of Forest Industries of BC (COFI) was formed, I was asked by M & B to work there as a staff member. I agreed to do so under contract through my consulting company. Shortly thereafter, American lumbermen launched a crusade to restrict the export of Canadian lumber to the US. I was dispatched to Washington, D.C. as a vice-president of COFI with instructions to examine the situation and locate lawyers to represent us. The COFI president at that time was J.R. Nicholson, a lawyer of distinction, the former chief exec-

utive officer of Brazilian Traction Company and a future lieutenant governor of BC.

At the time I went to Washington, Nicholson was engaged
in a dispute with J.V. Clyne, who as head of MacMillan Bloedel
demanded that the plan of defence in Washington be ignored.
Clyne had no reason to believe the COFI staff would accept his
veto, as he did not have one to exercise. In a dispute that took
place as a shouting match on the steps of the Vancouver Club,
Nicholson resigned his post. In fact, he did so with great glee,
because Prime Minister Lester B. Pearson had just invited him
to enter federal politics as Canadian minister of forests, and
Clyne had just made it possible for Nicholson to resign from
COFI without being in breach of contract. I resigned my own
position on the principle that COFI staff members should only
accept policy directives from the properly constituted board of
directors.

T.N. Beaupre, chairman of BC Forest Products and chairman of COFI, telephoned the next Sunday requesting that I
withdraw my resignation. I declined, saying I did not have a
contract of service and I had my own business to look after, as
well as clients awaiting attention. Beaupre, a forceful executive,
disclosed that Bert Hoffmeister, who had become BC's agent
general in London after leaving M & B, was available to accept
an appointment as president of COFI but wanted to know if I
would stay on as vice-president. Beaupre then appealed to my
sense of patriotism. "The American effort to damage BC's
exports must be headed off, and Bert and you can do it."

My response was forthright. Beaupre had challenged me and
I put the ball back in his court. M & B was the biggest financial
contributor to COFI, I said, and Mr. Clyne had created the
problem. If M & B, therefore, would support a substantial
increase in my fees, I would stay until the tariff board hearing
in Washington was completed.

So it was that Hoffmeister and I organized a defence of
Canada's export interest in Washington. Industry funding

came from Canadian sawmillers west of Ontario and US lumbermen who imported Canadian lumber. I acted as field man
to assist our counsel in Washington. Leading senators and
congressmen in the US were supplied with information and
their support was mustered. Here was I, a boy from Chilliwack,
registered as a foreign lobbyist in the American capital.

Whenever it was appropriate, Hoffmeister spoke to American groups, ranging from Chambers of Commerce, to export-
import associations, to Daughters of the Republic — indeed,
anyone who might support unrestricted Canadian and American lumber trading. Hoffmeister, articulate and physically
impressive, had the background that flag-waving Americans
love. He had been a civilian soldier who volunteered to serve
his country in battle, and had risen from captain to major
general strictly on merit. The Americans knew he was not one
of their typical stuffed shirt, West Point generals. With these
qualities he swayed American public opinion in frequent visits
to Washington and other American centres. He sold good will
and a reasonable argument.

Meanwhile, I prepared data to help our American lawyer
present our case. The game plan had three objectives. The first
was to keep politicians out of the dispute, which was not easy
with John Diefenbaker as Canadian prime minister. The second was to obtain the support of the American Home Builders
Association, key Democratic senators and other American
agencies known to favour unrestricted trade between Canada
and United States. The third was to represent Canadian interests at hearings in front of the American Tariff Board.

There was a desperate need to keep federal and provincial
politicians from sounding off, unless they used a script support-
ive of the plan in Washington. Williston kept a button on the
lips of headline-seeking politicians in Victoria. I went to Ottawa, as did Hoffmeister, to request a discreet silence from
federal politicians. We achieved freedom from political game-

playing, which gave us a chance to mount a professional presentation to the Tariff Board in Washington.

One event, however, nearly derailed us: the 1962 US senate elections. President Kennedy wanted Democratic senators to be elected in the timber states—Washington, Oregon and the Southern pine area. To attract votes, he intended to show sympathy and support for American lumbermen by requesting that Canada volunteer to curtail shipments of lumber to the US market. Kennedy's staff alerted our American lawyer. This gave us time to organize a diplomatic counterattack. First we met with Howard Green, then Canada's secretary of state for external affairs. Several plans of attack were designed. One was a face-to-face meeting with Senator Henry Jackson, a known friend of Canada and senior senator from Washington State. Green arranged for me to meet him in Seattle the next day, and the senator agreed to delay his return east for our meeting. He instructed me to make use of his office in Washington, D.C. and agreed to arrange an immediate meeting with President Kennedy's White House staff for our Washington lawyer.

A few days later, the lawyer and I met with a staffer from President Kennedy's office in a basement room of the White House. The staffer had the imposing title "Chief of the Canadian Problem." The three of us drafted a statement from President Kennedy for delivery to Prime Minister Diefenbaker. It was made to sound like a furious complaint against the Canadian practice of flooding the American market with low-priced lumber, but it was actually meaningless political jargon aimed not at Canada, but at lumbermen in Washington and Oregon. For the political effect the American president wanted, Canada would have to respond in a particular way.

I boarded an overnight flight to Vancouver and delivered a copy of the statement to Hoffmeister. Two days later, Hoffmeister was in Ottawa to meet with Diefenbaker and persuade him to respond as we had agreed in the basement of the White House. Diefenbaker, confined to his residence with a sprained ankle, was the lone occupant of a huge room furnished with only a desk and a chair. He was obscured by a mountain of files of every description, heaped in disorder on the desk and the floor. After hearing Hoffmeister, Deifenbaker raged at the perfidy of President Kennedy and threatened retaliation — everything short of open warfare, and even that exclusion was uncertain.

As patiently as possible, Hoffmeister pointed out the need for diplomacy. He argued that the Canadian response, drafted with the aid of White House staff, would quiet politicians south of the border and enhance the Canadian presentation to the US Tariff Board. In the end, Hoffmeister out-talked Diefenbaker. This was a gargantuan achievement, made possible by his urgent plea to keep politics and politicians out of the tariff hearing in order to rely on points of American law.

Diefenbaker then demanded a description of the legal position and finally expressed his satisfaction. He could not, however, be swayed from adding a one-liner to the return message to the White House. Hoffmeister, his patience wearing thin, volunteered to carry the draft response to the clerk of the Privy Council for immediate dispatch. He felt confident the clerk would agree to remove the offending sentence. After discussion, the clerk said it was impossible for him to alter the words of the prime minister.

Undaunted, Hoffmeister persisted, pointing out several words that could be crossed out and several that could be added. The clerk abruptly left the room as if in response to a call of nature, and Hoffmeister pencilled in a few word changes that would mean a gold mine of support. The clerk returned, reached for the telephone and read the statement to Diefenbaker. The Chief, not having a copy of his original version and no longer on stage in front of a man from Vancouver, listened and approved it without comment. Hoffmeister's version was sent to President Kennedy. No bones were broken, no blood spilled and no egos bruised. The tariff hearing was not impaired.

The lumber dispute of 1962 went before five senior American judges. We had a solid, highly professional defence. H.P. Pogue, my old sidekick and master forest surveyor, also became a secret weapon. He went before the US Tariff Board and explained that BC managed its forests on an even flow, sustained yield basis. Therefore, it was impossible for BC mills to increase the annual production of lumber and flood the American market when demand increased. This was a thin argument, but Pogue made an able, convoluted and charming presentation to the American judges. The court ruled unanimously in favour of the Canadian lumbermen. The American press described it as a "Bloodless Pearl Harbor."

Some twenty-four years later, in a repeat of the "American Lumber Problem," Canada did not fare so well. Canada lost for two reasons. The first was that the monopoly in control of timber in BC was indeed shamefully subsidized through underpriced stumpage, "sympathetic administration" and other forms of support by the provincial government. The second was that Canada's defence was dealt within the political arena. In the end, Pat Carney, Canadian minister of international trade, obtained a useful compromise by facing the truth about BC's underpriced stumpage. She persuaded the Americans to convert the inevitable tariff barrier into a surcharge on Canadian lumber exports. This ensured the money went to the provincial treasuries in Canada, rather than into the US treasury. Our industry negotiators, on the other hand, were prepared to see $1 billion per year of public equity disappear across the border, rather than admit to the underpriced stumpage levels provided in BC.

Following the conclusion of the tariff fight, I left COFI and returned to the contracting and consulting business. Throughout the 1960s and most of the 1970s, the big companies used their base in the Tree Farm Licences to extend control over timber rights in the remainder of the public forests. Theoretically, this land was to have been left for independent loggers and sawmills to buy through the competitive bidding process. Not only did we encounter, in our contracting work, the consequences of the growing monopoly, but I began to get an increasing amount of consulting work from citizen businesses that were being squeezed by the corporations and their ambitious managers.

Since the establishment of Tree Farm Licences, citizen business has been restricted to operating in three areas available to it. The first is logging, essentially under contract to the monopoly. The second is primary manufacturing in coastal sawmills, plywood operations and shake and shingle plants, which operate mostly without an assured supply of logs. These plants rely on a log market controlled by the monopoly. Sales of chips and residues to pulp mills are controlled by the monopoly, which also sets the prices. The third area available is secondary manufacturing, producing mouldings, panel stock, shelving, trusses, prefabricated housing, fencing and similar products. These manufacturers also obtain their raw lumber from the monopoly.

An example of the challenges faced by these businesses is the situation one of my client sawmills encountered in its contract to buy an annual quantity of Douglas fir logs. The agreement was to buy the logs at a structured price linked to the selling price of Douglas fir lumber. The supplier therefore increased the selling price of the logs every time lumber prices increased. There was no reduction when lumber prices declined. The difficulty was aggravated by the fact that my client had to sell his hemlock chips to the supplier at 80 percent of the posted Vancouver chip price. Government restrictions prevented him from selling his chips in the US, where prices were double the BC rate.

For a period, as a representative of the non-pulp sector of the coastal sawmill industry, I attended meetings of Forest Industrial Relations, the group that negotiates labour contracts with the International Woodworkers of America. The pulp sector companies were experiencing a strong market demand and wanted to stay at work. They needed to avoid a loss of their pulp log and sawmill chip supply. Jack Munro, the IWA president, had an armful of leverage in the negotiations. He was not giving an inch, and the pulp majors had told him they would surrender. That, in turn, required that the majors convince the non-pulp companies, which I represented, to accept Munro's demands.

At one of the crucial meetings in the negotiations, I told the pulp people I would recommend that my clients vote against the pulp sector's wage package. We would force a strike at our operations. I announced that I had Munro's assurance the IWA pickets would block deliveries of logs and chips to the pulp mills.

There was a silence around the table, accompanied by annoyed frowns and the clearing of throats by representatives of the major companies who operate pulp mills. A recess was taken while they called their head offices in Toronto, Tokyo or wherever else control of their companies happened to reside at that time. The chairman of the industry negotiating committee, an operator of several pulp mills, asked me to join him in the hallway, where he asked, "Ian, what is it you want?"

I told him that my clients wanted an increase in pulp chip prices before agreeing to Munro's wage and benefit package. The pulp guy let loose with a tirade of insulting remarks, and then assured me the chip price would be increased so the strike could be averted. Interestingly, this raised the Vancouver price of chips to just half that paid by the pulp mill in Bellingham, only a few miles across the border. Out of curiosity, a few months later I checked the stumpage appraisal documents issued by the Forest Service for three of the companies operating pulp mills. As I had expected, the stumpage charged for payment to the public treasury had been reduced to offset the wage increase to the IWA.

Effectively, so-called independent logging businesses lack access to a free and open timber supply. They operate at the sufferance of and subject to the abuse of the monopoly in respect to log supply, the disposal of pulp chips and, in some instances, access to offshore markets for lumber. Through these mechanisms, the profit of citizen business is plundered.

The interior forest industry has, in a practical sense, no log market. Citizen business conversion plants that have a timber supply are in a serious squeeze. The price paid for chips by pulp mills, which are units of the monopoly, is less than the cost of extracting the equivalent log volume from the forest. The pulp economy draws its raw material from the forest, via the sawmills, at less than the cost of production. The sawmills bear the cost of silvicultural crop replacement while the pulp mills, with their massive profit levels, ride free of such obligations. The government collaborates in this legalized banditry by allowing a surplus of chips which prevents the sawmills from raising chip prices.

There is no other country in the world that structures forest policy to give its pulp and paper industry a free ride. This is a dangerous practice if we expect to continue exporting pulp products under free trade. The purchasing countries in free trade zones are unlikely to tolerate this form of subsidy. The Americans would be justified in imposing a countervailing duty on raw pulp and manufactured pulp products entering the US market. BC should not be surprised if such a countervail is introduced. This is particularly true as ownership and control of the pulp companies operating in BC moves away from the US. It is what will accrue to the voters, who have elected and sustained the current provincial government since 1975.

Very early in the history of Tree Farm Licences, independent loggers began to dwindle in numbers, and now they have all but vanished. They cling to life through the contractor clause in TFL agreements that orders 50 percent of allowed annual harvest from publicly owned lands within a Tree Farm Licence to be harvested by independent loggers. Ambiguous and inept language in the legislation and regulations reflects the reluc-

tance of officials in the Ministry of Forests to recognize the
rights and the role of independent loggers. They are still viewed
as intruders in the warm embrace shared by the monopoly's
professional foresters and the government's professional foresters. It is an attitude fostered by Orchard, who wrote in his
memoirs that "there is no role for the independent logger. We
must allocate timber to existing industries which already have
made themselves fundamental factors in the economic life of
the province." Defending the TFL system, Orchard argued,
"Forest management finally was possible in BC because of. . .
consolidation of forest properties into big holdings in the hands
of wealthy and well-financed big companies and corporations. . .
and so, big forest business and forest management came to BC,
and the small logger found himself on the way out. He squealed
like a stuck pig. . . ."

Orchard did not know, or he chose to ignore, that the logger
has to be a silviculturalist, just as a farmer is an agriculturalist.
Orchard's elitist, bureaucratic attitude set the stage for removing locally based, independent businessmen who had a powerful built-in incentive to care for the forest on which their
livelihoods depended.

For four decades or more, independent businessmen have
been at the mercy of a monopoly aided and abetted by employees of the government bureaucracy. It has taken until the
beginning of 1990, for example, to bring about the inclusion of
an arbitration procedure to settle contract disputes between
licencees and independent loggers. And in spite of years of
promises to increase the portion of the provincial timber harvest sold at competitive auctions to 25 percent, there is still a
free market in only 7 or 8 percent of the cut.

The monopoly is less than enthusiastic about the contractor
clause, an attitude demonstrated by numerous deceits over the
years. At one time the operator of TFL 1 employed the Canadian National Railway to haul logs and chips to the Prince
Rupert pulp mill. The rail costs were classified as log produc-

tion costs and the CNR was claimed as a logging contractor. Once, after MacMillan retired, MacMillan Bloedel formed a joint venture company which it controlled and operated as a logging contractor.

Since they began consolidating their control over the forest, the companies that form the monopoly have had to play a careful game. On one hand, they want to put the squeeze on local business, and on the other they want to avoid paying a fair price for public timber. This situation is created by the stumpage appraisal system that determines the selling price of public timber, because of the lack of a free, competitive timber market in BC. The appraisal system determines stumpage to be the selling price of logs (on the coast) or lumber (in the interior), minus operating costs and an allowance for profit and risk. The Forest Service does not insist on using actual logging costs in these calculations, but uses theoretical figures provided by professional foresters working for the big companies. The selling price is derived from the Vancouver Log Market and is largely artificial. The monopolies realize great benefit by paying contractors as little as possible, and report exaggerated logging costs through the appraisal process, along with under-stated sale prices. Almost all of this activity is performed with the knowledge and approval of professional foresters, in clear violation of the Magna Carta principles of forestry.

CHAPTER 15

Independent Local Business Destroyed

In my role as industrial consultant, from time to time I was engaged to help local business through waters made stormy by the monopoly. The monopoly's member companies have "money managers" in faraway highrise towers in Toronto, New York, Tokyo or Wellington. There are subordinate money men ensconced in Vancouver highrises. Few have had rain in their lunch buckets; some have never even seen a forest. They are hired as messenger boys.

Let me expand my view in the following hypothetical scenario. The names as well as the events are fictional.

The Tree Farm Licence management and working plan is a contract setting out operations for the following five years. But suppose that unilaterally, and without warning, the money manager in New York decrees that the road building budget is to be cut in half. The money manager in Vancouver, the messenger boy, tells the company's chief forester he must reduce his road construction in Tree Farm Licence "Green Shoes" by one half.

198

The forester says, "I just signed the new five-year management plan with the Ministry of Forests. We are required to build roads in a particular sequence and location to comply with the silvicultural plan."

The senior money man in New York says, "To hell with silviculture and roads. We need money for a new development in Chile. You get what I give you and no more. We pay you to blow bubbles at the BC Forest Service. You have done it nicely for eighteen years and you have five more to go before retirement. Do I need to draw diagrams for you?"

The forester swears under his breath, genuflects to the local money manager and returns to his drafty office in the garret. He fusses and fumes, thinks about retirement, then telephones his logging contractor, who builds all the roads and logs the timber in TFL Green Shoes.

"Say Joe, that cutting plan and road program I told you was approved is going to be amended. I know I told you to gear up for twenty miles of roads for each of the next five years. Well, that's been cut back to only ten miles. Hell! What's that you say, you've already bought another backhoe and three gravel trucks? I hope you didn't get the tractor. You did! Darn it all, you should have checked with me first. Well, I know I told you the Forest Service had issued approvals and it was a go situation. No! No! The Forest Service has done its job."

The forester decides he needs support, so he asks Tom, vice-president of logging, to listen in on another telephone. Tom declines, saying, "You peddle him the BS. When I deal with him I do not want to know what you have discussed."

The forester returns to the phone. "My company wants to curtail capital expenditures on roads. Joe, keep your voice down and give me a break! I know roads are a cost of log production, not a capital expense, but that's the way the guy in New York classifies it. No, you can't talk to him. Joe, please cool down. I'll get back to you and work this out. Thanks, old buddy."

Then the company forester telephones the appropriate official in Victoria. "Andy, I want you to fix up the new five-year plan in Green Shoes. Yes, that's the one you signed for me in a rush the other day. Well, we now want to experiment with some long-yarding, using equipment my contractor designed. I don't want it getting around, but in future we're going after such intensive recovery that we can avoid slash burning. Soil will be opened up for easy plantation work at low cost.

"What's that you say, Andy? You like the plan because the government rebates stumpage to slash burn under Section 88? My friend, I give you my assurance, my company does not charge one dime more than our costs. Now Andy, this is what I want you to do. I will send you a logging plan with a reduced road layout that is designed for the new logging system. Will you sign your approval immediately? Good. Will you instruct your district office in Port Harry to waive inspection? Yeah? Thanks, old friend. Now Andy, because this change in road plan is an experimental application of long-yarding, until we get the system functioning, will you give me a letter waiving close utilization? Hell, Andy, I don't want to go to Harry to plead a case for waiver. They'll tie me up with a field inspection."

The forester puts the telephone down, blows his nose, brushes an eyebrow, then returns to the conversation. "But Andy, damn it, you have overruled them before on the minister's orders. Do you want me to talk him? OK, OK! Don't lose your cool! You'll give me the waiver? You do understand I need that waiver immediately? Good stuff, and thanks, Andy."

The next day the forester goes out to TFL Green Shoes, his first visit in fourteen months. There he meets with the contractor, "Joe Old Buddy."

"Joe, we're going into a new plan. I've decided to cut back on roads. It means you'll be yarding 1200 feet with some long corners, but we only want standard logs—no small wood or Y & Z grades, and just the best of the X grades. Other than that, we'll operate as normal. The Forest Service has approved the new plan and it's the one that will apply in your contract."

Joe's voice rises in alarm and anger. "We are going to talk about a rate increase. I have to do all the work of falling, bucking and trimming small wood and X, Y and Z logs. I have to leave them in the slash and get no return for my work. My daily production will fall with long-yarding and the hangups on logs left in heavy slash. Reduced daily production costs me money. Yes, and slash burn will be difficult, expensive and risky with all that fodder on the ground. You're damn right we have to talk about costs. I have road equipment idle, and it's equipment you told me I needed for the next five-year logging plan. In fact, you ordered me to get it. Who in hell ever gave you a waiver to waste close utilization logs in the slash? This is bush league and it comes out of my pocket. You get sympathetic administration from your friends in government, and I get shafted."

"Joe, Joe, old buddy, cool it. I'm just the forester. I make the plan. Tom is the logger and he'll deal with rates. He has a problem because he's under orders from New York that logging rates to contractors cannot be increased this year. You know I'll recommend an upward adjustment. After all, in this new plan I've saved the money needed for roads. Also, just between you and me, I got Andy in the ministry to leave the stumpage at close utilization levels. That means we get the big logs out at the lower close utilization stumpage rate. That's big money, Joe, and I would like to see you get some of it. I promise to do my best for you, old buddy."

But the forester doesn't do a thing for Joe. And Tom, the company's vice-president of logging, stonewalls the rate adjustment, pointing out that the contract required Joe to log in accordance with the plan approved by the Ministry of Forests. Tom says, "Joe, Boy, you're stuck. Either log on those terms, or I cancel your contract."

"You son of a bitch," Joe roars. "I am not your Joe Boy. That forester of yours had the ministry amend the plan. The Forest Service in Harry tells me they were overruled and not even allowed to make an inspection. You people have set me up."

"Joe, *boy!*" Tom says coldly. "You have worked for us for twelve years and you are able to go to Palm Springs every winter. Are you going to accept this deal or not? If not, I cancel right now. I will also tell you that if you make any allegation that we positioned the Forest Service to get a deal and set you up, I will see to it you never work in this industry again."

Joe, his bank loan overdrawn, his equipment financed and personal guarantees placing his home and his personal equity at risk, capitulates. His logging costs increase 19 percent due to the change in work specifications. That costs him roughly $150,000 per year for five years. He has to sell off road building equipment at a loss of $350,000. The heavy slash results in a fire that Joe has to fight at a cost of $75,000.

The change in specifications is, in fact, a breach of contract by his employer. The employer is sheltered by a clause in the contract that links Joe to accepting the cutting permit approved by the Ministry of Forests, sight unseen.

This setup allows Tom to use the charade that the Ministry of Forests amended the logging plan and that the company, like Joe, was contractually bound to log in a manner specified by the ministry.

Joe appeals to the minister of forests, outlining the flagrant waste of public property and the corrupt stumpage appraisal procedures. These procedures denied the public treasury proper payment on the big logs recovered, under the pretence of being an experiment. The experiment, however, was nothing more than reversion to a long-yarding practice which had been abandoned two decades earlier when mobile yarders and loaders became available.

The minister, hearing Joe's complaints, accuses Joe of trying to make trouble. Joe is then sent to see Andy, who discloses the change in logging specifications has been solicited by Joe's employer. Andy says that he refused them, but was requested by the minister to approve the management plan changes and find a method to lower the stumpage. Andy concludes, "I can't afford to lose my job."

Suspecting he had been lied to, duped and milked by the money manager and the political process, Joe might come to me for advice. All I could say is, "You are not alone. I know of many who feel as you do. Charge this to experience, and in future let me see your contract before you sign it. We'll have your lawyer rewrite it so the hot shots in New York can't milk you like they did this time. You did not really have a contract. You had a piece of paper with open-ended wording that set you up. As for the Forest Service, they are part of the problem. In my opinion they have lost their ability to deal in the public interest, much less in fairness to citizen business."

Joe is fictional, but he puts me in mind of a real logger, this one a supplier to a sawmill in Nanaimo. His tale of woe involved a timber sale he had obtained at a public auction of mature timber on Tree Farm Licence 2. When this licence was granted to Crown Zellerbach in 1949, all the mature timber on it was left outside the licence for the small, independent loggers to cut. My new client was logging under the Small Business Enterprise Program, set up by the second Bennett government as a sop to the citizen business logging community.

He was paying $43.40 per hundred cubic feet stumpage to the public treasury for cedar he was logging at the top of a mountain, and the market for cedar logs had collapsed. At the bottom of the same mountain, Crown Zellerbach had just received a downward stumpage adjustment of $12.00 to a rate of $12.83 per hundred cubic feet, for cedar of higher quality growing less than two miles from an ocean booming ground.

"Small business timber sales are not permitted stumpage adjustment," I told him. "Only companies with Tree Farm Licences or other tenures guaranteeing an annual supply are allowed that benefit."

204   THREE MEN AND A FORESTER

The logger responded, "But if I have to pay stumpage at three and a half times what the TFL holder pays, I lose money. If I do not log, then my timber sale is cancelled. The timber will revert to Crown Zellerbach for minimum stumpage, and they get free use of the roads I build. They'll make a pot of money. The government takes my roads and gives them to Crown Zellerbach, free of charge."

"I am sorry I can't help you," I replied. "Employing me would be wasting your money. The forest policy is stacked against independent business. You pay a penalty to be an entrepreneur in your native land."

This discrimination against independent business is built into the Forest Act. Ministry of Forests documents reveal one-sided procedures that provide favours to the companies allocated Tree Farm Licences, and give the back of the hand to independent so-called small business in the forest industry.

After 1975, executives in the Tree Farm Licence companies developed a conviction that nothing was beyond their entitlement. In 1981, several companies forming the monopoly called their logging contractors in and ordered them to fire their unionized workers and employ non-union workers at reduced rates of pay. The contractors were also ordered to eliminate benefits such as holiday pay, pension contributions and free room and board. The savings would be passed along to the Tree Farm Licencees. The contractors were also told to adopt a policy of leaving close utilization logs in the slash. This was an abandonment of public equity and a cost burden on the contractors, who would not be paid for the work they put into those logs. After a concerted effort, the contractors and the union fought off this blatant attempt to hijack both their own income and the public treasuries.

This procedure is known as "externalizing costs"; that is, unloading them onto someone outside the company. The monopoly in control of public timber externalizes with ease and relish. The task is performed by middle managers, in many cases professional foresters, whose positions in their companies are enhanced by such devotion to duty. A company has been allocated public timber. The manager contracts out road and bridge building, logging and trucking of logs, each described as a phase. He preaches the virtues of private enterprise, although he has never established or run his own business, met a payroll or faced bankruptcy. The manager seeks out an earnest young man and provides him with a phase contract requiring $600,000 of equipment and two employees. The earnest convert to private enterprise runs the machine and his wife works nights on maintenance and lubrication. The manager pays him for piecework, denying him capital cost allowances, interest on his investments and depreciation when he negotiates the contract price. The convert works overtime at no cost to the company, and pays for repairs to his machinery. His personal assets are mortgaged and he has a demand loan at the bank. If he complains, the manager prattles on about the free enterprise system and lets him know there are lots more where he came from.

This same skillful exercise in contract administration is used in the silviculture business. A manager discusses a tree planting contract with a young couple, recent forestry graduates. Instead of a straightforward bidding process, the manager offers a rate based on "acceptable costs." He is holding similar discussions with two or three other contractors for the same job, and eventually talks the young couple into the lowest rate. The budding entrepreneurs hire a crew and buy their equipment and supplies, even though the manager has not been able to provide them with a written contract, which is mysteriously held up in the accounting office. Once they are committed, the manager tells them, regretfully, that his boss won't approve the agreed-upon price, and either it must be reduced further or the job must be cancelled. They reluctantly agree to a 10 percent reduction.

In the couple's frenetic rush to survive, seedlings get planted in rotten logs, bogs and rock piles. The manager makes them replant enough to pass Forest Service inspection, at their expense, although 50 percent or more will never survive. By this time the earnest young couple are working twelve hours a day, seven days a week. They have been suckered into the company's cost externalization scheme.

The manager gets brownie points from the company, which uses some of the money saved to help pay for ads that convince the public what a great job the company is doing in the public forests. What the manager probably doesn't know is that most of the money saved in the "externalization" exercise is invested by the company in a pine plantation in some underdeveloped country. This plantation will be ready for harvesting in fifteen or twenty years, they say, just at about the time the cream has been skimmed off the BC forests and the pulp mills have worn out.

As a second-generation forester, after fifty years of professional experience, I am saddened and sorry to report that this is the way it is. And it is not as if we were not warned. Thirty-five years ago, H.R. MacMillan said that it would be a sorry day when BC's forest industry consists of a few big companies holding most of the timber, "to the disadvantage and early extermination of the most hard working, virile, versatile, and ingenious element of our population, the independent market logger and the small mill man."

CHAPTER 16

Sympathetic Administration

Very early one morning in 1969, my telephone rang. A voice with a heavy New York accent asked me to join him at breakfast. It was Abe Meltzer, a lumber wholesaler serving the US Atlantic coast market. Abe had started in business as a truck driver on the Brooklyn docks. With unusual energy and dedication, he had founded Triangle Pacific Forest Products Ltd., one of the largest buyers of BC lumber for sale along the east coast of America.

"I buy shiploads of lumber to supply my customers from Miami to Boston," he explained over coffee. "The BC producers are jacking me around on prices. I want you to work for me and I'll buy my own production capacity in BC."

He paid me a finder's fee, and in short order his ample chequebook allowed me to obtain three sawmills and a timber supply.

Somewhat later, I went to Central America to do some work for the United Nations forestry section, on assignment to write the forest law for the Republic of Honduras. On travelling

207

through New York on my way home, I paid a courtesy call to Meltzer, who insisted I go to work for him. He said the managers of the mills I had bought for him — the former owners — all wanted to quit to clip coupons, and he needed a chief executive officer. He made a proposal that involved buying out my share of Millstream Timber and selling it back to my two partners. He was so persistent in his offer that I said I would make my own deal with my partners. He then offered me an appointment as a director and vice-president of his New York company. He offered 2,000 shares of treasury stock in the company for each year of service, plus a more than generous salary. I signed on for five years and converted my share equity to an important capital fund.

During this period, Bill Bennett became an MLA and sought the leadership of the Social Credit party. I happened to meet W.A.C., no longer premier, walking through the lobby of the Empress Hotel in Victoria. He suggested I join him for a cup of tea, and then asked me to support Bill in the forthcoming leadership convention. I agreed, and in due course received a succession of invitations to political meetings where Bill Bennett was the speaker. Attending were just about every senior executive from the forest industry. During the cocktail hour, talk centred on contributions to Social Credit political funding. One objective was to provide a standby fund on the expectation that in the next election, Bill Bennett and the Social Credit party would form a minority government. The standby fund would allow Bennett to call a snap election, timed to catch the NDP off guard. I didn't like the idea, and as a representative of a foreign-controlled company I did not feel the company should participate. I do not know whether the fund was ever raised.

At that time, my company shared ownership of an executive aircraft with another forest company. The aircraft was made available to Bill Bennett from time to time before he became premier, so I occasionally travelled with him, and very much enjoyed discussing forestry with him. After he became premier I met with him on two occasions, at his request, to discuss forest issues. When the Forest Act was given a major overhaul in 1978, I told him the draft statute had serious flaws. I said his party's proposed reorganization of the Forest Service would make it impotent. I was not invited to meet with him again.

As I look back now on the events since 1975, it is clear that I was right, and that the damage to the forest, the public equity, was even greater than I had anticipated in my pessimism. Developments in forest policy in the eleven years that the Bill Bennett and subsequent Social Credit regimes have been in office, rank among the worst in the province's history. The public agencies administering forest laws violated or circumvented their own laws. This encouraged the forest companies, whose tentacles dominate the tenures on public timber, to abuse every tenet of forest management. The excuse for this behaviour, involving politicians, civil servants and employees of industry, has been that almost anything was acceptable if it would keep the NDP from getting back into power. The argument persuaded a lot of otherwise decent people to become involved in a massive violation of the public interest. That it enabled many major forest companies to make large amounts of money was a convenient bonus for them.

I became aware of what was going on through some work I did for one of my clients, a logging contractor. His contract obligated him to fall and buck all the trees within a designated area. Some months after he began work, the first scale and royalty accounts from the Ministry of Forests were available to him. He was appalled to discover a large shortfall in income payable to him, and he engaged my services. In examining his data, I noticed there were almost no X, Y and Z grade logs in the official scale report. Roughly 25 percent of the timber he had felled and bucked was not recorded. As a consequence, he was not being paid for work performed, and the public treasury was not being paid for its timber. Public property had been allowed, indeed ordered, to be wasted in the slash.

I raised the matter with my client's employer, a Tree Farm Licencee. The manager I talked to berated me for being a meddler. I listened to his insults for a moment, then said: "Just for the record, from this point I am no longer working to collect a fee from my client. I am now going to devote my time to discover why you, as a professional forester, treat my client in a manner inconsistent with your duty as a professional forester." I asked him why he had abandoned public property in the form of X, Y and Z grade logs, and refused to pay my client after he had done all the work of falling the trees and bucking the logs. "I remind you that these are statutory grades, specified in his contract with you."

The forester spluttered a few moments before answering. "My controller ordered we make no payment for X, Y, and Z grades. There is nothing I can do."

Next, I called on the controller and told him he was in breach of contract. He shrugged his shoulders and replied that he got his orders from a senior official in Toronto. The controller, a reasonable man clever enough to pass the buck, disclosed the existence of a waiver from a senior official in the Forest Service, which absolved his company from having to pay my client. I disagreed, saying the issue was a matter of contractual law. It had nothing to do with a waiver involving a deal between his company and the Ministry of Forests. My client had fulfilled his contract. In due course the TFL company conceded, and settlement for my client was obtained, but certainly not easily.

Pursuing the matter further for my own satisfaction, I went to Victoria and visited an assistant deputy minister, a professional forester. He confirmed that the statutory log grades had not been amended, and said there was no universal waiver authorizing the waste of any grades of logs. I then asked him what waiver the TFL company's controller was talking about. Who had authorized it, and why?

"I can't say why," the nervous assistant deputy said. "But I will show you a form letter that went out to the attached list of companies."

The letter he showed me was signed by T.M. Waterland, minister of forests at the time. It had been delivered to a list of chief executive officers, almost all representatives of companies with Tree Farm Licences. It read:

> I have been canvassing. . . the forest industry. . . to determine the status of various sectors. . . . I must at this time again remind Tree Farm licencees that they have a heavy socio-economic responsibility that goes far beyond managing their firms and the timber lands of the Tree Farm Licences.
>
> I would ask that you consider the following: The Ministry of Forests is dealing with your company in a sympathetic administrative manner. Are you treating your contractors in the same manner and is this management style being carried out at all levels of your company?

This was my first direct contact with the notorious policy of selective "sympathetic administration" from which certain forest companies benefitted during the economic recession of the early 1980s. It had been initiated, I learned later, in an earlier memo sent to senior Forest Service managers on October 1, 1981. After reference to the financial plight of the industry, it concluded: "We must be prepared to practise some sympathetic administration while meeting our responsibility to the Crown. We can use the velvet glove approach instead of a ten-pound sledgehammer. Instead of automatic suspensions, we can use individual contact to find out what the situation is and work out a solution and still obtain our objectives."

This policy had no legal status. It simply instructed the bureaucrats in the ministry to ignore, on a selective basis, the laws of forest administration. It was a vaguely defined program that allowed the waste of public property. This, in turn, resulted in a greater consumption of high-grade logs, an expanded pace of logging and increased federal and provincial subsidies for reforestation. Had these memos and letters been made public and the policy of sympathetic administration been debated on the floor of the legislature, it is doubtful the government could have survived the next election.

In many ways, sympathetic administration was an attitude. It became so pervasive that it still survives, even during the most profitable period in the industry's history. The policy was the final straw for US lumber producers, who were already upset about the hidden subsidies granted Tree Farm Licencees. It compelled the Americans once again to seek a tariff on Canadian softwood lumber entering the US.

While it can be argued that the industry required some relief during the recession, this under-the-table deal with certain, favoured companies is indefensible. Its worst effect may have been that it turned large numbers of otherwise honest professional foresters into agents of deception, dealing a final blow to the already shaky ethical foundations of the profession. Sympathetic administration extinguished the last spark of the Magna Carta forest ethic.

After leaving Victoria, I went back to examine the affairs of my logging contractor client more closely. His contract obligated him to burn slash at his expense and his risk, in the event that the fires escaped and damaged private or public timber. His employer, the Tree Farm Licencee, had invoiced the public treasury for the slash burn, claiming it was a silvicultural expense and eligible for a stumpage rebate. That scam was not enough, though; the Tree Farm Licencee also invoiced the contractor for supervision, aircraft patrols and other items said to be costs incurred for the slash burn. When this was all wrapped up, the contractor paid the costs of the slash burn, both his and those of his employer. The employer, a multi-national company, then turned around and charged the public treasury. This too was sympathetic administration at work.

Throughout this period, in the course of my work, I was able to examine many documents revealing a variety of ways that the public interest was being violated. A benefit enjoyed by some companies involved the issuing of invoices for stumpage and royalty accounts. Under previous policy, invoices for stumpage due the Crown were delivered along with official scale reports, at intervals of thirty days, and required immediate payment. During this period, however, one of my clients learned that invoices for the timber he had cut for a TFL company were being withheld by the Forest Service, to be paid twice a year, in April and October. The effect of this was to grant the licencee an interest-free line of credit, partly at the expense of the public treasury, which had to delay the collection of its receivable, and partly at the expense of the contractor, who had spent a large amount of money fulfilling his logging contract. This contract specified he would be paid when the official scale reports were received from the Forest Service.

While dealing with the sympathetic administration problem, I dropped in to visit Alex Fraser, the MLA from the Cariboo and the Social Credit highways minister. I had first met him when I worked in his riding running a sawmill and logging operation.

I called on him in his Victoria office late in the afternoon. He withdrew a bottle of Scotch from a desk drawer, handed me a portion, and put his feet up. We talked about the Chilcotin country, an environment he loved. I told him what I was uncovering about the sympathetic administration policy.

Alex growled. He told me he had been out visiting a community with a crossroads store that he had long promised would be served with a new highway. This time the residents refused to talk to him in civil terms.

"What have I done to deserve this?" Alex had asked.

"You built a road three miles away," someone told him. "Now we are a backwater."

Surprised, Alex had responded, "I did not. We are under a restraint program and your road had to be deferred. Nobody else is going to build roads in my riding. Where is this road?"

They took him to a point west of town where, running west towards the coast mountains, was a magnificent new road.

Alex was visibly angry as he told the story. "That goddamn Forest Service. While I am denied money, those guys withdraw it through the back door by rebating stumpage. This never gets looked at on the floor of the legislature or by public accounts."

Alex finished his drink and poured another in agitation. "That Forest Service has run amok, it is out of control. We as a government are going to pay a price one of these days. Not only will we get defeated, but we are liable to be run out of town on rail like a bunch of carpetbaggers."

As I have described, coastal scaling procedures were cheating contractors and the public out of revenue as early as the 1970s. The major licencees refused to scale logs at the point of origin, first towing them in booms to sorting grounds and storage areas in Howe Sound. The loss of low-grade logs from sinkage was of benefit to the licencees because they didn't have to pay the higher costs of processing them. The harvest of these logs was not calculated into the allowable annual cut. In 1971, the contractors appealed to Ray Williston, who was forest minister. He began to act, and then the government changed. By the time the NDP government figured out what was happening, they were voted out and Waterland was in as young Bennett's forest minister.

In 1975 the Truck Loggers Association, on whose board of directors I sat at the time, made a vigorous appeal to Waterland for the mandatory use of dryland sorting grounds. The Ministry of Forests agreed with us, and over the next few years, dryland sorts were put in place all over the coast. Some companies, including M & B, adopted weigh scaling systems in which the logs were bundled and weighed before being placed in the water. Random bundles were then selected for measurement to maintain an accurate correlation between log weights and volumes. Others set up quite a different system, designed so that the initial scaling could not be checked.

One of these was built by BC Forest Products at Shoal Island, near the company's Crofton pulp mill. Logs were brought to this site by contractors, either with trucks from southern Vancouver Island logging operations or by water in bundled truckload lots that would prevent sinking of heavy or low-grade logs. Five major coastal contractors were shipping their logs into this sorting ground, including one I was associated with.

When the first scale reports on logs moving through this operation were received, it was apparent something was wrong. All experienced loggers develop their own methods of accurately estimating truckload volumes, which are constantly verified by official scales. This time, though, the volumes reported were 10–12 percent lower than they should have been. The Shoal Island dispute erupted.

Individually, the various contractors began discussing the shortfall with BCFP. One contractor asked a senior BCFP official in 1981 if any other contractor had complained about the scale, and was told "No". In fact, when we obtained internal BCFP documents, we discovered every contractor had complained consistently from the day Shoal Island started operation. The contractor also asked at the time if regular check scales had been done, and was told they had. In fact, only one check had been done and it showed an underscale.

When this contractor visited Shoal Island and observed how his logs were being scaled, it was clear to him what was happening. In a proper scaling procedure the truckloads would be kept together as measurable units. No logs would be bucked, and the operation would be conducted so that a check scale could be done. At Shoal Island, the truckload bundles were being broken up and spread out on the ground, so the loads were mixed up before they were scaled. Logs were being broken into two or more pieces by rough machine handling. Lengths shorter than 12 feet were then being bucked off the logs. By convention, such short lengths are classed as "chunks" and are not scaled. These chunks were being sold or taken, without scaling, to BCFP's Crofton pulp mill.

The Shoal Island sort, like several others, was set up as a high-production operation. Scaling requires the careful measuring, counting and recording of logs. At Shoal Island the scalers, who are trained and licenced by the government, had to rush to measure the logs in the midst of a noisy, dirty industrial operation. Because of the pressure on them not to impede production, they were organized in a manner that caused them to miss logs. They did not have time to record properly their measurements or counts, which they attempted to do later in a noisy, crowded shack on the site. It was impossible for them to check their work without slowing production.

In 1979, the Forest Service did a check scale that showed an original scale of 2,086 logs had missed 171 pieces and was low by 7.1 percent in volume. Then the Forest Service made a "mistake" in documenting the check, and it was reported as being within one-tenth of a cubic metre of the original. When BCFP kept insisting there was nothing wrong with scaling, we brought in an independent scaler. He found a 12–16 percent shortfall in the official scale.

By this point I had been hired as a consultant by all the Shoal Island contractors. After further, lengthy discussions with BCFP, my clients were offered a settlement of 6 percent of logs scaled for a portion of the time concerned, on the condition they sign a waiver of further claims. All except one of the contractors decided to accept this offer. The exception was Percy Logging, a company of long service to BCFP in Knight Inlet, which had decided to end its contract at the end of 1980. However, a large quantity of Percy's logs were, in fact, scaled in 1981. He protested and claimed compensation for his 1980 production. He was essentially told to drop dead. He then sued BCFP for breach of contract: the clause requiring BCFP to "cause all logs to be scaled," and ultimately obtained a court recommended settlement.

The Ministry of Forests had still made no attempt to collect the stumpage shortfall that resulted from flawed scaling. This was despite BCFP's admission of at least part of the shortfall in its compensation offer of 6 percent. On behalf of my clients, I presented requests for an official investigation to the Ministry of Forests, the deputy minister and the minister. Very soon I was warned that if I didn't drop the whole matter, a strong possibility existed that I would never work in the industry again.

That threat motivated me to turn the whole matter over to Ombudsman Karl Friedmann. He immediately seized the appropriate documents from the Forest Service, including a critical file from an assistant deputy minister's desk. After a thorough study, assisted by scalers and other experts, the ombudsman concluded that my clients and the public treasury had been consistently cheated at Shoal Island. He recommended the Forest Service do a reassessment as provided for in the Forest Act. He also named other dryland sorts where the same situation prevailed. One after the other, all the accountable professional foresters and senior officials in government turned down his requests. Friedmann took the extraordinary step of issuing a special report to the legislature.

For his efforts, Friedmann was viciously attacked on the floor of the house by government MLAs, and described on occasion as "Comrade Karl." In the end, Friedmann's contract was not renewed.

The legislature was kept in the dark about what was really happening. Internal reports of the Ministry of Forests, not made public but later obtained in evidence, showed that immediately after the correction of scaling procedures at Shoal Island, there was a 12–15 percent increase of scale per truckload processed. This information, however, was not reported to the Minister of Forests. An unsigned letter was sent to the minister on May 19, 1983, from the accountable official in the ministry. It purported to explain the situation at Shoal Island, but neglected to mention the recent scale increase. This unsigned letter misled the minister and the entire legislature.

In 1986, Percy's case against BCFP, and that of my other clients against the Ministry of Forests, went before Chief Justice Allen McEachern in an unusual court procedure called a "mini-trial." Ignored by the media and not widely reported, it heard seventeen days of testimony without cross-examination. In it, the chief justice explained he would outline the ruling he would give if it were a real trial.

At one point, to prove how much timber had disappeared, I hired one of the province's most respected forest consultants to go to one of the logging areas and measure all the stumps in the clear-cut. With this data, I arranged for a computer model to be created that reconstructed the forest my client had logged. When the log volumes contained in this area were compared with the scale, it was evident that the highest grade first and second logs from a large portion of the trees were missing on the scale sheet. The result was a gross underscale of the most valuable public property.

Through a time-consuming and expensive examination of documents, the chief justice confirmed an underscale throughout the years Shoal Island had operated. He confirmed the conclusions of the ombudsman who had been so cruelly condemned on the floor of the legislature. In dealing with the negligence charge against the ministry, the chief justice was faced with the forest ministry's defence that representatives of the Queen can do no wrong.

BCFP decided to settle out of court, agreeing to pay Percy $1.5 million. The other suit against the ministry was not clearly resolved, and would have required my clients to launch an action that could have carried on to the Supreme Court of Canada. In lieu of assuming that burden, my clients accepted sufficient compensation to pay their legal bills. Those contractors who were prepared to trust BCFP again received new five-year contracts with important safeguards written in, one of which was an arbitration procedure to be used in the event of a dispute.

During the course of the mini-trial, large numbers of documents had been subpoenaed from the Ministry of Forests and BCFP, and part of my work was to go over them. Even after a lifetime of working in the forest industry, I was astonished at the degree of mismanagement. Both in concept and procedure, Shoal Island violated every step in scaling law. It spawned a massive underscale, seriously damaging to both public and contractors' equity. With the exception of a single occasion, no check scales were done by an accountable Ministry of Forests official until late 1981 when the whistle was blown by one of my clients. Scaling procedures at three of the five major dryland sorts on Vancouver Island were not operated in accordance with scaling law.

It is difficult to understand how such conditions could be tolerated by senior Forest Service officials and field staff, all whom are well-trained and understand their accountability to superintend scaling. Yet the situation at Shoal Island and other dryland sorts was tolerated for years. One is led to speculate that a signal came from a higher authority that inspections, including check scales, would not be appreciated. What Shoal Island exposed was the disposition of the Ministry of Forests to give the back of the hand to independent and local business, while rushing around to protect the special position of those companies with Tree Farm Licences.

It would be interesting to know whether particular companies, such as those operating the offending dryland sorts, were generous donors of political money to the Social Credit party. If so, it is possible that Ombudsman Friedmann hit a nerve in his investigation of scaling, and that it was for this reason he was attacked from the floor of the legislature.

There are many sad and outrageous aspects to the situation that has developed, particularly since 1975. One is the plundering of the public purse. It is difficult to calculate how much public equity has been lost by under-assessed sales of public timber, under-measure of public property and other manipulations of the fixers, whose ranks now include foresters who have abandoned the Magna Carta ethic. One former forest minister has estimated it is in the neighbourhood of $1 billion a year, another suggests it is double that. If one compares stumpage and log prices collected on public timber sales in BC with those in the US and others on a global timber market, a $1 billion dollar reduction in public revenue seems reasonable. Some of this shortfall has been collected during the last couple of years, thanks to the efforts of the US lumber producers who threatened to collect a tariff on our lumber if we didn't come to our senses and begin collecting it here. It is a sad commentary on the state of our politicians, our government, our professional foresters and the executives who run the industry that our foreign competitors must introduce a measure of honesty into our system.

The failure of government to collect this equity is responsible for our budget deficits during the Bill Bennett regime, for the deficiencies in our education system, health care, social services, highways and other services. It is why we have to pay such high taxes. And, most important of all, it is money we should be spending on tending future crops so that our children and their children can maintain a decent standard of living in this province.

CHAPTER 17

What to Do

From my youngest days, when I rode on my father's shoulders, my life has been bound up with the forests of British Columbia. My whole working life has been devoted to the forest industry, from my job as a lowly spark chaser on a railway show, to a stint as the chief executive officer of a large forest corporation. On occasion, it has been my duty as a professional forester to advise forest ministers and the premier of the province on matters of forest policy and practice.

Never, it seems to me now, have British Columbians been at such a critical point regarding our forests. For more than forty years, we have been living with the flawed forest policy of the tenure system. For the past fifteen years, that system has been manipulated by a small group of fixers employed by a handful of corporations owned and operated from a distance and, in terms of the welfare of our forests, by the most irresponsible government the province has ever had. In the past year we have seen mills attached to Tree Farm Licences shut down because of a shortage of timber. Many local economies are crumbling,

EMPLOYMENT & VALUE ADDED IN B.C.				
	1961	1971	1981	1987	% Change, 1961–1987
Forest Industry Production ($ Millions)	$1,886	$3,066	$3,453	$4,680	+248%
Gross Provincial Product	$13,649	$23,613	$39,526	$43,448	+318%
Percent of GPP by Forest Industry	13.82%	12.98%	8.74%	10.77%	-22%
Volume Logged (M³)(cubic metre)	33,045,76	56,550,915	62,625,000	89,052,000	+269%
Total Value to Provincial Economy per M³	$57.07	$54.22	$55.14	$52.55	-8%
Forest Industry Jobs	65,677	78,343	86,848	85,000	+29%
Jobs / 1000 M³	1.99	1.39	1.39	0.95	-52%

and the residents of these communities are increasingly engaged in bitter conflicts over how to use the remaining forests.
There is an anger building, of the sort that H.R. MacMillan
foresaw in 1956 when he spoke to Commissioner Sloan: the
reaction that "would occur if, in the next generation or sooner,
the smaller enterprisers and working people, and their friends

awoke to the realization that a very large proportion of the Crown timber. . .was forbidden ground, held by a few big companies."

The Vander Zalm government, with no idea of what it wanted except to stay in power, attempted to carry out the ill-advised forest policies dreamed up by the previous administration. All of these policies were designed to strengthen the existing corporate structure. Public outrage stopped the creation of a vast new Tree Farm Licence empire. Now a cumbersome forest commission will try to decide what to do about forest tenure and other matters.

We also face hard decisions about how to manage our second growth forests, the new forests that have regenerated naturally or been planted after logging. If we proceed in the direction we are going, we will clear-cut these forests at younger and younger ages, feeding the timber into new and bigger pulp mills, allowing our solid wood plants to wither and die. If we do this, we will condemn ourselves to a future of land use conflicts, unstable local economies and, eventually, declining productivity of forest land.

We have a choice. We can adopt a whole new approach. Following the European method, we can put tens of thousands of people to work tending the forests, carefully extracting timber and limiting our clear-cuts to small areas. If we take this route and concentrate on growing high-value timber for manufacturing, we will create even more jobs and be more successful at sustaining local economies. Our choice is between a labour-intensive, diversified forest industry, with a pulp and paper industry existing on the waste produced by the higher value manufacturers, and a capital-intensive, pulp-dominated industry making the first claim on timber and treating the forests as high-volume, low-value commodities.

If we are going to take control of our forests and our future, there are a few basic decisions we must make. First, control over forest administration must be placed under regional land

COMPARISONS–1984				
	Volume Logged (Million M³)	Value of Forest Product Shipment (Million$)	Value / M³	Direct Jobs	Jobs / 1000 M³
B.C.	74.56	$10,390	$139.36	78,174	1.05
Other Canada	86.31	$22,419	$259.75	189,739	2.20
U.S.	410.03	$176,661	$430.85	1,456,100	3.55
New Zealand	5.27	$3,041	$577.22	26,351	5.00
Sweden	55.96	$13,586	$242.82	140,900	2.52
Switzerland	7.00	$7,593	$1,084,66	79,900	11.41

(All Values in Canadian Dollars)
Sources: B.C. Ministry of Forests Annual Reports; Statistics Canada 25–202; B.C. Economic Accounts; U.S. Forest Service: Timber Sale Information Reporting System

use boards that answer to the communities in each region. The goal of these boards would be to develop and protect sustainable local forest economies. The boards would make decisions about resource use in their regions, not simply give advice to the bureaucrats and fixers in Victoria or Vancouver who have been ignoring local interests for the past forty years.

The regional boards would be responsible for taking into account the interests and concerns of all forest users in their regions. They would have to guarantee that the forests are managed to sustain the economies of the region, rather than practising "Uclueletization," which sacrifices the future of one community for the sake of another. The economy of almost every community in this province is dependent on the forest that surrounds it. Now, the fate of those communities lies in the hands of fixers working for the corporate monopolies and government bureaucrats in Victoria. We need to protect not only the jobs of the people in these communities, but the investments in homes, businesses, schools, hospitals and other infrastructures that our citizens have made. Those who have experienced the death of a town due to an industry withering and dying, will have a particular understanding of this need.

The regional boards, as well as the forest users and the provincial government, must be guided by a fundamental forest law that applies to all forest land, public and private. This law will say, as simply and clearly as possible, that it is not permissible to mistreat forests. The law will recognize that forests, no matter who owns them, are vital to the environment and the economy of a much wider area than the particular piece of land they occupy, and that the entire community has an interest in their welfare. While this kind of public right over private property might seem like a drastic measure in this country, it is a common policy in countries with well-managed forests.

Probably the most important decisions we have to make are concerned with tenure. We must first abandon the policy of maintaining public ownership of forest land and leasing it to private interests. Forty years of the Tree Farm Licence system has shown us this approach is not working: it has created a system in which no one is responsible for the forests of the future. We need to diversify our tenure. A portion should be owned and managed in small units by individuals or families, as is the case in our agriculture industry and much of the forest land in more advanced forest nations. We also need some larger private ownerships, particularly in areas remote from settlements. It has been demonstrated in other parts of the world, as well as here, that some of the best forestry is practised in corporate forests. Some forests must remain in public ownership, to be managed by the provincial Forest Service or a similar body. These public forests would include those that serve important public functions in addition to the production of

NET PUBLIC REVENUES			
Volume Logged (M³)	Total Revenue	Total Expenses	Net Revenue/ M³
All U.S. National Forests 54,231,539	$1,776,662,550	$908,763,570	$16.00
U.S. National Forests on B.C. Borders 13,442,661	$356,840,640	$215,320,950	$10.53
B.C. Public Forests 80,008,000	$536,287,000	$534,913,000	$0.02
(All Values in Canadian Dollars) U.S. Figures for Year 1988–89, U.S. Forestry Service B.C. Figures for Year 1987–88, Ministry of Forests Annual Report			

commercial timber, such as municipal watersheds, unique environments and recreation areas.

It may be difficult to determine just how much of the province's forest lands should be placed in each type of tenure, but there are responsible models for us throughout the world. In other countries, a third of the forests are in small private holdings, a third are in larger private or corporate ownership and a third are in public ownership.

This kind of change would allow us to abandon the Tree Farm Licence system that is serving us so poorly. Because TFLs are only leases, governed by regulations that are constantly changing, licencees are not motivated to do anything beyond what is absolutely necessary to retain their tenure. TFLs actively discourage the practice of silviculture. They foster the bending of rules, the pursuit of short-term profits and the corruption of people who work on them. We would be far better off to take them away from the corporate monopolies now holding them and turn them over to the people now employed on them as contractors, so they can be managed as independent forest farming operations.

This action may seem like a drastic and radical step, but it is not. Any major company primarily interested in manufacturing forest products and marketing them internationally will be far more successful if it buys its timber from a motivated, efficient and secure community of locally based forest managers. In the long run, the most secure timber supply can be provided by a large number of stable, independent citizen business forest owners dedicated to the business of growing and selling timber. The best, most efficient use of the big, integrated forest corporations is in certain phases of wood-product manufacturing, such as pulp and paper, and marketing. They are inept and inefficient at operating in the woods. Moreover, their present control of forest tenure is the source of almost all their conflict with the public. Most people now employed by the big corporations operating the TFLs would be far better off working for companies they own themselves, selling the timber they grow in a free and open log market. Most of the large corporations holding TFLs and other tenures in BC operate manufacturing plants and, even now, are building half-billion-dollar mills in other countries where they buy all of their timber on the open market.

The only real losers in this kind of tenure change would be the people who have benefitted from an unsound forest management policy. We need a separation of those who manage the forests and produce commercial timber, and those who use this timber to manufacture products for sale around the world. The point of separation should be a log market — not the controlled, manipulated Vancouver Log Market, but a real market of many buyers and sellers. It is this market that will insure the growing of high-value timber crops, as well as the manufacture of high-value forest products. This market will ensure sufficient revenue to those in the business of growing and selling timber.

	Industrial Forest Area (Million Hectares)	**% Owned by:**			
		Public	Corporate	Small Private	Other
Norway	7.5	18%	—	75%	6% (commons)
Finland	22	23.6%	7.4%	65.3%	3.7% (commons)
Sweden	23.7	26%	25%	49%	—
France	13.7	12%	—	70%	18% (commons)
W. Germany	7.2	31%	25%	44%	—
Yugoslavia	—	40%	—	60%	—
U.S.S.R.	890	90%	—	—	10% (commons)
Japan	26.4	32%	—	57%	11% (commons)
U.S.	500	28%	13%	59%	—
Canada	198.4	92%	— 8% —		—
B.C.	48.2	99%	— 1% —		—

TENURE

It will also provide the manufacturers with the grades and species of timber they require, at prices lower than they are paying now.

Benefits from these kinds of tenure changes will also accrue to foresters and to the profession of forestry. For forty years there have been only two employers of young foresters, the major integrated companies and the Ministry of Forests. In this kind of employment situation it is unwise to say what one thinks. The motto of the professional forester in BC could well be "Don't rock the boat." People who follow this rule long enough eventually stop thinking. When that happens to foresters, they lose the ethical direction they were granted with the signing of the Magna Carta.

If we had many forest owners and some diversity in tenure types there would be many different jobs, employers and professional opportunities open to foresters, as there are in other countries. If BC foresters were freed from the requirement of keeping their mouths shut and their minds closed to everything except the prevailing corporate or bureaucratic line, the practice of silviculture in this province would make a great leap forward.

This is no small issue: it is the very key to our future. The well-being of our communities, both ecological and economic, is directly related to the fate of the province's forests. If they are poorly managed we will be impoverished. If they are well-managed, the business of silviculture will attract the brightest and best minds of future generations. This cannot occur if the primary qualification for a professional forester is to make himself subservient to the short-term goals of corporate money managers and political manipulators.

I grew up believing, I worked all my life believing, and I still believe, that in this province the highest goal to which a person can aspire is that of the professional forester as protector of the realm. If we are willing to change our forest laws, that responsibility of the forester will be realized in British Columbia once more, and our magnificent forests — critical to our economy and to our very survival — will be cared for in the way that all present and future British Columbians deserve.

Appendix

In 1955–56, along with professional foresters A.P. MacBean and Keith Shaw, I assisted H.R. MacMillan in preparing his submissions to the 2nd Sloan Royal Commission on Forestry.

MacMillan predicted that the Tree Farm Licence system would destroy the forest and drag down the province's economy. He foretold that "annual allowable cut" would soon become a numbers game involving inflating the mature timber inventory and overstating growth of the new crop. He also saw the potential for selective political interference in the Tree Farm Licence system and attempted to ensure that all dealings in public property would be open to scrutiny.

The attached 55 points summarize the views that MacMillan presented to the Royal Commissioner.

SUBMITTED TO ROYAL COMMISSION ON FORESTRY, BRITISH COLUMBIA BY H.R. MACMILLAN, CHAIRMAN OF THE BOARD, NOVEMBER 3, 1955, VANCOUVER, B.C.

Summary of Recommendations

The numerous recommendations we have offered are summarized hereunder:

(1) The policy of "sustained annual yield" of forest crop to be maintained and extended throughout the province.

(2) No more Forest Management Licences to be granted in Vancouver Forest District.

(3) A copy of each Forest Management Licence contract to be on file and available for public reference in the office of the District Forester for the District.

(4) That all details of every issued Forest Management Licence be published promptly in the Official Gazette.

(5) That the stumpage fixed yearly for each Forest Management Licence be published promptly in the Official Gazette.

(6) That logs cut from Forest Management Licences, if suitable for peelers or good fir and spruce sawmill logs, shall not be used for pulp.

(7) That Licensees integrate their converting mills within a reasonable time.

(8) That Forest Management Licence contracts shall be changed only by mutual agreement.

(9) That Forest Management Licences be reduced in area if the mills of the Licensee cannot use the full crop.

(10) That Government establish an Insurance Fund to protect Licensees.

(11) That the Forest Service prevent Licensees from logging the most profitable tracts more rapidly than the poorer.

(12) That the 30 percent clause be put in all Forest Management Licence contracts if opportunity arises.

(13) That every practical incentive be given to log "salvage" before it is lost through burn or decay.

(14) That any dams on the Fraser River provide for safe transport of logs.

(15) That no Forest Management Licences be issued unless the Licensee contributes thereto all the timber owned by him as required by Section 33 of the Forest Act.

(16) That the condition be moderated requiring the Licensee to protect and replant at his cost, Government Forest for 90 years.

(17) All Crown Forest not in temporary cutting tenures be added immediately to Public Working Circles.

(18) The boundaries of Public Working Circles be subject to change only by the Legislature.

(19) All temporary cutting tenures revert to Crown as soon as the first crop of merchantable timber is removed, as was the intention of the Act.

(20) That second growth in areas of one square mile or more be surveyed out from areas held by one firm under temporary cutting tenures and added to Public Working Circles.

(21) That all provisions of the Land Act and the Forest Act preventing alienation of Crown Forest land be maintained.

(22) That all suitable land acquired by Government in the Esquimalt & Nanaimo Railway grant be made a Public Working Circle.

(23) That Public Working Circles be administered as separate units.

(24) That a Forester be appointed to manage each Public Working Circle.

(25) That access roads be built to permit market loggers to reach inaccessible Crown Forests.

(26) That money be borrowed to build access roads provided the tolls on Forest products will liquidate the borrowing.

(27) That the crop on Public Working Circles be not sold until it has reached the age of greatest annual return.

(28) That as high a standard of management and protection be maintained on Public Working Circles as the Forest Service requires on Forest Management Licences.

(29) That the Forest Service retain and use a sufficient amount of revenue from Timber Sales to re-establish Forest crops on not sufficiently restocked Crown land in the Forest District producing the revenue.

(30) That every feasible means be adopted to keep in business the market logger particularly in the region of the Strait of Georgia.

(31) That the Vancouver market price be paid to market loggers for logs delivered at every railhead and at every integrated mill, or mill protected by reserves of Forest Management Licence timber, whether on railhead or not.

(32) That the principle of the Silvicultural Fund, as practised East of the Coast Mountains, be adopted in Vancouver Forest District.

(33) The blackmail frequently practised at Timber Sales be prevented.

(34) That Vancouver Forest District be divided into two Forest Districts.

(35) That all administrative Foresters spend 60 days in the Forest each year.

(36) That the Faculty of Forestry at University of British Columbia produce more Foresters who will work in the Forests.

(37) That Government of Canada contribute more money yearly under the Canada Forestry Act to the protection and research of British Columbia Forests.

(38) That sufficient of the Forest revenue be used to protect, establish, and study our Forests.

(39) That the Forest Service strengthen its fire protection force.

(40) That the Game Act allow the destruction of game found destroying Forest plantations.

(41) That the open season for deer and grouse in Vancouver Forest District does not begin until fall rains start.

(42) That there be devised a means of appeal beyond the Minister's decision, and beyond the Lieutenant-Governor In Council.

(43) That slash burning be modified where possible.

(44) That the machinery for Forest closures be speeded up.

(45) That Government placard and patrol Forest roads to support logging firms in fire protection.

(46) That a broader policy be undertaken by Government and Forest Industry to educate Public respecting Forest management.

(47) That Government does not discriminate against Forest Industry when taxing natural resources.

(48) That the practice of using chips and salvage logs for pulp be extended as rapidly as possible.

(49) That a fund be established by Government and Forest Industry for Forest Research at University of British Columbia.

(50) That in the interest of maintaining exports Forest Industry should try to buy a larger volume from the sterling area.

(51) That British Columbia strengthen the Forest Service.

(52) That British Columbia do not appoint a Forest Board or Commission to administer the Forests.

(53) That the offices of Deputy Minister of Forests and Chief Forester be separated, each to be held by a Forester.

(54) That a Provincial Advisory Board be appointed.

(55) That export of unmanufactured Forest products from British Columbia is contrary to Public interest and should be restricted.

Index